BOUNCE

DOWN IS INEVITABLE

UP IS A CHOICE

Tyler,

Best Wishes!

CHAD VARGA

This book is dedicated to my loving family—Kristie, Cameron, and Kiersten—for your endless support and encouragement. Special thanks to: the Marcy and Brian Martin family for your friendship and faithful commitment to run this race with us; the Margo and Larry Bean family for your uncommon wisdom, support, and advice; the Mari Ann and John Martin family for your generosity and belief in me; Scott and Judy Reichard for your early support and patience throughout this project; Karen Smith Haskins for catching the vision and running with it alongside us; Doug Combs for being more than a pastor—for being a true friend; and Jody Eversole for being a trusted advisor and faithful friend from the beginning.

WHAT STUDENTS ARE SAYING

"Chad, I cannot tell you how moved I am by your book. I can completely relate to your story. I never met my dad and my mom is an alcoholic and drug addict. She always told us she never wanted us and that we were the worst things that ever happened to her. She left my brother and I a couple of years ago. We have been in three different foster care homes and I have always felt like giving up and that no one cared about me. This may sound weird, but I know you care. Thank you. I will never forget what your book has taught me."
JASMINE, 9ᵀᴴ GRADE, VIRGINIA

"I have never liked to read...actually, I hate it. I heard you speak and had my mom buy one of your books for me because I wanted you to sign it for me. On the way home I started reading it and I couldn't put it down. I read the entire thing that night. It has given me hope that I too can be the first in my family to go to college."
ALEJANDRO, 6ᵀᴴ GRADE, CALIFORNIA

"Chad, I just wanted to let you know that your book Bounce has completely changed my life. It is by far the best book I have ever read. You are my hero."
RYAN, 10ᵀᴴ GRADE, MASSACHUSETTS

"Chad, I have been bullied all my life for being different. I guess being 'emo' is not cool to some people. It got so bad that I thought about suicide and I never told anyone, not my parents or my friends. I really wanted to let you know that because of you I have stopped thinking that way and have opened up to my parents. You have helped me more than you'll ever know."
JAMES, 9ᵀᴴ GRADE, GEORGIA

"I personally want to thank you for everything you do. I have heard you speak twice and just finished reading Bounce. You have inspired me more than anyone or anything ever has. To know what you've been through is heartbreaking, yet you've pushed and fought and believed to get where you are today. That's unbelievable. Thank you Chad Varga."

ALEX, 8TH GRADE, FLORIDA

"When I was four, my younger brother died. It was right after that my parents got divorced. My dad started doing drugs and still is and my mom could care less about my life, she only cares about her boyfriends. Last month I started getting really depressed, but I always kept a smile on my face at school. I started feeling like my life didn't matter and started cutting. Then I was given your book. I feel like you wrote it just for me. Because of you, I have stopped cutting and will NEVER give up!"

BRITTANY, 9TH GRADE, ILLINOIS

"I know I am just another kid with another message but I want you to know that you have changed my life. I was at your assembly and I couldn't take my eyes off you. I listened to every word you said. That was the most incredible story I've ever heard. I thought that it would be something boring but you proved me wrong. I was shocked the way you grabbed everyone's attention. It impacted me greatly and changed everything about me. It has made me a better person. Today I have realized I want to help kids all over the world just like you do."

JOHN, 11TH GRADE, MARYLAND

"I feel like I'm a different person with a new perspective on life. Your book has showed me that no matter how hard things get, if you never give up, there's hope."

ALYSSA, 8TH GRADE, KANSAS

"I can honestly say you have opened my eyes! You are the best speaker our school has ever had. Every eye was on you and nobody spoke the whole time. Every one of my friends was holding on to every word you spoke. Thank you for coming and believing in us."
LAUREN, 12TH GRADE, PENNSYLVANIA

"Wow! All I can say is that your book was completely inspiring. I'm positive you are impacting millions of people. You have shown me that I am capable of accomplishing great things with my life and I want you to know that you are the most inspiring person I have ever met!"
TAMIKA, 7TH GRADE, CALIFORNIA

"Your speech really inspired me. I cried almost the whole assembly. I am really going through some hard times. My parents just got divorced and I've been giving in to some peer pressure from friends. I just wanted you to know that you put a smile on my face and reached me today and not a lot of people have ever done that for me."
BRIANNA, 9TH GRADE, WEST VIRGINIA

"That was one of the best things that has ever happened to our school. It was amazing and I'll never forget your speech. I needed to hear that. Just forty minutes changed a lot of people's outlook toward life."
NICOLE, 10TH GRADE, CALIFORNIA

"Chad, you are incredible. Best assembly we've ever had! I never knew that one hour could change our whole school."
ROB, 12TH GRADE, OKLAHOMA

"Chad, thank you for coming to our school today. I loved every minute of it. I can kind of relate to you because my mom was on drugs real bad and she overdosed because she

was sick of us. It's been real hard on me this past year. I lost my dad and my grandma. Thank you for talking to all of us. Because of you, I will never give up."
JACKSON, 8TH GRADE, ILLINOIS

"When I heard we were going to have an assembly, I thought it would be the typical boring kind. Little did I know how wrong I was—as soon as you started speaking, I knew you could understand what I was going through."
STEPHEN, 11TH GRADE, INDIANA

"Thank you for your speech today. It has really inspired me! I don't have problems at home but I have had problems at school with boys telling me bad stuff and treating me bad. I have tried to run away and I even tried cutting myself. I realized today that I want to be successful no matter what people say and you taught me that! You are truly inspirational and you are amazing for doing what you do and giving me hope!"
SERENA, 8TH GRADE, MISSISSIPPI

....

WHAT EDUCATORS ARE SAYING

"During my thirty-plus years in education I've never seen an audience as riveted by a speaker. You are the best speaker I've ever had and I have been recommending you to all the principals I know."
PRINCIPAL FROM PENNSYLVANIA

"In all my years at this high school, we have never had anyone connect with our students like you did during your talk. They were still talking about your visit several weeks after you had gone."
PRINCIPAL FROM FLORIDA

"Chad Varga is the most outstanding speaker I've ever heard. He had our students spellbound for forty-five minutes. They were in awe of his life story."
PRINCIPAL FROM GEORGIA

"No one has ever held the attention of our students like you did today. I was concerned that it would be difficult to hold the attention of so many but you had them spellbound with the honest way you tell your story. You made a lasting impression that our students will never forget."
SUPERINTENDENT FROM TEXAS

"Your message was powerful and by far the best for students I have ever seen. I was truly amazed at your ability to captivate the attention of our entire student body. Our students will apply the life lessons they learned in your sixty minute presentation for the next sixty years."
PRINCIPAL FROM KENTUCKY

"I have been in public education for almost thirty years. I have attended countless assemblies. I must say, I have never been in the presence of a speaker than captivated the attention of everyone in the room like you and your stories did."
SUPERINTENDENT FROM INDIANA

"I recommend Chad Varga with great enthusiasm, completely assured that he will change, impact, influence and make a definite difference in the lives of our youth throughout America."
ASSISTANT PRINCIPAL FROM MARYLAND

CONTENTS

0

THE CHOICE

THE CHOICE

Imagine you are standing alone in the center of a basketball court. In your hands is a basketball. Now imagine extending your arms straight out from your chest and dropping that ball. What would happen? The ball would bounce to about the same point from which you dropped it, right? Sure, if it was a little deflated, it wouldn't bounce quite as high. And if it was overinflated, it might bounce a little higher. But either way, the ball would hit the hardwood floor and spring back up to about the same point from where it started.

Now imagine raising the basketball above your head with both hands and throwing it down with as much force as you can muster. What would happen then? That ball would bounce two, three, maybe even four times higher than you. It's the principles of physics at work. The harder a ball is thrown down, the higher it will bounce.

Now imagine that hardwood floor is life, and that basketball is you.

Like a basketball court, life can be shiny and inviting. It can also be very hard. If circumstances throw you down, life can seem unfair and unforgiving—unless you're made of material suited to bounce, like a basketball. If you are, you can turn the hard knocks of life into a launching pad. And the harder you are thrown down, the higher you can bounce back up.

This isn't just a metaphor. It's one of the most important truths of your existence and mine.

We all stand on the hardwood court of life. It beckons us to come and play. Have fun. Follow your heart.

It also reminds us that all is not fun and games. Life can be hard.

We are all thrown down during the course of our lifetime. If it happens when you are young, it can seem incredibly unfair. Unfortunately, you and I cannot always control when or why we are thrown down. We can only control how we react. This is the choice no one on the planet can take from you—ever. No matter what happens to you, no matter how long it happens, you alone can choose how you will respond to the circumstances of your life.

Some people choose to live their lives like a deflated basketball. When they are thrown down to the hardwood, they stay down. They spend their days angry, blaming others for what happened. As a result, they cannot bounce back up and fulfill their dreams. They often end up becoming the very opposite of who they once hoped to be.

Others choose to live like an unused basketball.

They've seen glimpses of their potential, but they're so fearful of disappointment, rejection or failure that they spend their days immobilized and powerless, unable to take the necessary steps to elevate themselves off the ground. They are so afraid of being thrown down that they never rise up and reach their potential.

Fortunately, there are also those who take life for what it is—a physics lesson in their favor. They get thrown down like we all do—sometimes even harder and more often than most. But every time they hit the hardwood, they use the downward force to spring back up—higher and higher. The harder their mistakes or circumstances throw them down, the higher they reach up.

They know what every highly successful person has learned along the way. Down is inevitable. Up is a choice. They choose to bounce.

You can too.

I will show you how.

Chad Varga

June 1, 2013 / West Chester, Ohio

1

DREAMS AND REALITY

DREAMS AND REALITY

In my early years, I was thrown down.

A lot.

I grew up in a part of the country where basketball wasn't just a way of life. For many young people, it was a way to stay alive. Some of the greatest names in the history of the NBA can trace their success to an obscure patch of asphalt in the shadow of a run-down factory or housing project. That seemed to be my destiny too. It didn't hurt that I would grow to be 6'7" with size 17 shoes and a vertical leap of 41 inches. By middle school, my love for basketball had become a full-blown passion. I had a dream to be the first in my family to go to college, earn a degree and then play pro ball, and hopefully, have a family one day and give them a life that I never had.

We all have dreams when we are young and resilient and capable of extraordinary faith in our future. It's a time when we still believe that whatever we desire from life can become a reality one day. The truth is, that reality never changes. What does change is that as we grow older, we begin losing our faith in our dreams.

Somewhere along the way, this thing people call "reality" hits. Suddenly you realize that your circumstances are not connecting the dots to the future you imagined. Maybe your parents are divorced and you have no money or you've been abused or you are not the right size or color or gender or...fill in the blank. For whatever reason—and there are always reasons—what you dream of doing and what you believe you can "really" do become two very different realities. Others' comments often fuel this belief.

They begin asserting things like, "You can't do that," and, "You need to live in reality," and, "That's impossible," and, "Maybe in your next life." The comments are occasionally from a place of good intentions, especially if family and friends are just trying to protect you from disappointment. But such comments do not convey the truth about you or your future.

The fact is that all dreamers, including the greatest achievers in history, have heard these same comments:

- Harrison Ford was told he couldn't act
- Oprah Winfrey was told she was unfit for television
- Michael Jordan was told he couldn't play varsity basketball
- Amelia Earhart was told she was the wrong gender
- Albert Einstein was told he would amount to nothing
- Anne Frank was told she didn't matter
- Elvis Presley was told he wasn't going anywhere

- Rosa Parks was told she was the wrong color

The difference between those who realize their dreams and those who don't is simple: Those who realize their dreams refuse to accept someone else's "reality" for their lives. They dare to keep pursuing their dreams despite the unfavorable odds and constant objections.

If you talk to successful people in any field of life, and you ask them the secret to their accomplishments, one of the things they say is, "It started with a dream inside of me that I couldn't shake, that just wouldn't go away. Once I finally grabbed hold of it as my own and ran with it, no matter how hard and difficult things got, the dream carried me through. It was the dream that allowed me to tune out the negative words of others and keep fighting."

Tragically, our world is filled with people who never rise above average. Look around—most people never stretch beyond their past and present circumstances. They never become the people they long to be. They never do the things they desire to do because they fail to lift their heads and see a bigger, brighter future. Average people have dreams like everyone else, but they become discouraged and disenchanted along the way. Ultimately, the choice they make about their circumstances is that it is easier to let their dreams die.

I understand—on a very personal level—why people make this choice. Life can be hard. In my case, it was brutally hard. I had every practical reason to let my dreams die. To be honest, I almost did. I nearly gave up more times than I can remember. But somehow, some way, I found just enough strength to keep going—even though there was a lot standing in the way of the future I desired; even though the forces fighting against me began opposing my dreams before I could talk.

In many ways, my circumstances were extremely unfair. The one thing that none of us gets to choose in life is the family that we are born into. Unfortunately, I was born into a home that was incredibly dysfunctional and unstable. I didn't choose to have a mother who was a violent alcoholic and drug addict, or for my parents to be divorced before I was three, or to be living in an unsafe and volatile environment, especially when I was a young child. And yet somehow I survived until I was old enough to do something about the circumstances—until I was old enough to make a choice to rise above the mess that continually surrounded me.

I'd be lying if I told you it was easy. It was never easy. The horrible circumstances of my childhood didn't suddenly improve when I turned a certain age. In some respects, they became much worse as I came to understand what sort of home I lived in and what sort of person my mom really was.

What did improve as I grew older was my understanding of the critical role I played in following my dreams. The more I saw the impact my choices had on my life, the more momentum I gained.

I eventually came to realize that I could take charge of what was happening inside me even if everything outside me was falling apart. The more I took responsibility and learned to rely on my inner strength, the higher I rose above my circumstances. The same will be true for you. It is not a matter of "maybe."

If you accept responsibility for your life and learn to rise up no matter how many times you're knocked down, you can reach your dreams. In fact, don't be surprised if you go even higher and further than you imagined. It's exactly what happened with me. That is the summary of my life.

I'm now going to tell you the full story, including the raw details of growing up in my broken home—even the dark secrets no child should ever have to endure, let alone share with others. When I'm finished, I'll then tell you what I learned about life and about what it really takes to make your dreams a reality. Here's a clue for now: it has nothing to do with where you live or how much money you have or how many people like you.

I want you to know that I don't take these things I'm about to share with you lightly. I hope you don't either. The details of my upbringing—if you can call it that—are not for the faint of heart. And I don't share them simply because they make for a great page-turning story. I share the details of my life because I know in reading them you will comprehend some critical truths about yourself. Most importantly, you will be reminded that you are more powerful than you probably realize. I'm not talking about the insecure swagger of a bully or the fear-based aggression of a manipulator. I'm talking about the faith and inner strength that rises up when you fully comprehend the impact you can have—in your own life and in the lives of others.

I know you have dreams. I also know your dreams have enemies—enemies inside you that insist you're not good enough or talented enough or deserving enough; and enemies outside you in the form of doubters, haters and difficult circumstances. Defeating these adversaries will require that you make tough choices—sometimes, choices that make your stomach hurt for days, and other times, choices that fill your heart with an inexplicable joy and peace. As you will see, I have experienced both ends of the spectrum. As you will also see, there is risk no matter what choice you make—to chase your dreams or let them die. But the greatest risk is in choosing to do nothing and simply letting life happen to you.

Dreams never come to you. They don't find you. If they did, we would all have everything we want. You have to chase your dreams down, grip them with both hands and never let them go. No matter what comes.
I know you can.

How do I know? Let me now tell you the rest of my story and you will understand. It is clear proof that you and I are not defined by how hard life throws us down; we are defined by how high we rise in response.

And there is no limit to how high.

2

LIVING ON DEATH'S DOORSTEP

LIVING ON DEATH'S DOORSTEP

I did most of my growing up in various broken-down houses and apartments in some of the poorest sections of the Detroit, Michigan area where drugs, alcohol and violence were prevalent in plain daylight. The signs only increased at night. I rarely got a good night's sleep as a child. The sound of fighting outside my window or the pop-pop-pop of gunfire was common. I was struck with so much fear on some nights that I slept on the floor of my bedroom. I didn't exactly grow up in an environment that bred success.

To make matters worse, we never stayed in one place very long. The reasons varied, but moving usually had to do with my mom's addictions or my dad being out of work and unable to afford a place to live. By the time I reached high school, I had attended seventeen different schools. Friendships were difficult enough moving from one school to another, sometimes more than once in the same year, but what made life most difficult was the circumstances surrounding my parents.

I was born twenty-three months after my older sister, Wendy, at a time when she and I still had two parents living under the same roof. This would change very early in my life—just before I turned three years old—but it would be a few years later until I understood what had happened and why.

The issue wasn't my father. He struggled to make ends meet from time to time, but he was a loving dad who always worked hard and did everything in his power to provide for us. The issue was my mom. In the early days, even my dad didn't know how bad-off she really was.

My parents had married young and, while my dad's love for my mom was true, marriage was ultimately a form of escape for my mom who was harboring demons from her own childhood that could only be silenced for so long. My dad was completely blindsided when my mom cheated on him six months after their wedding day. But as we all soon discovered, her unfaithfulness was only a symptom of a much bigger, more destructive pattern. By the time I was born, she had fallen deep into a lifestyle of drug and alcohol abuse. She lived in bars and spent many nights away from home. Despite my dad's attempts to help her, she spiraled out of control. Our family followed suit.

My dad didn't believe in divorce but became convinced that having sole custody of Wendy and me was the only way to shelter us from the danger of my mom's choices. The paperwork was filed, but he underestimated the courts, and my mom.

She showed up at the hearing clean and sharp as a tack. It was a time in our country where the courts predominantly gave custody to the mother when there was a divorce. My mom knew this and she convinced the judge that she was fit to raise us. To the shock of everyone who knew the truth about her addictions, she won sole custody. While my dad continued to petition the courts for custody, my home life went from an unstable two-parent home to an utterly chaotic single-parent home. Truth be told, I don't know that my mom was present enough to even call her a parent.

My earliest memories are of toddling around our house in only a diaper while my mom and her friends violently abused alcohol and drugs in the living room, kitchen and bedrooms. To this day there are still vivid scenes in my mind, like watching my mom mainlining—injecting heroine and cocaine into the main artery in her inner thigh.

Without my dad around, our house quickly became the party house. And what you have to understand is that when there's a party going on and there are little kids around, the kids eventually become a nuisance.

My mom's boyfriends used to mix hard liquor with Kool-Aid and give it to me to drink, hoping I'd fall asleep and stop bothering them. I even remember my mom calling me over to the kitchen table where she was drinking her long-necked beer. She would sit me on her lap and scoop beer suds into my mouth with a spoon. After I had just enough alcohol in my system to start feeling funny, she would hand me a bag of cookies and shoo me off to bed. I thought she loved me and was just giving me a treat. What I didn't know is that she too wanted me out of the way.

I was just a kid who loved to eat so I would shuffle back to my bedroom, climb into my bed and start devouring those cookies. To you that might sound like a treat, but all I remember is pounding those cookies without any supervision while the chocolate smeared on my face and the crumbs fell on my sheets and then, when I was full, dropping the bag of cookies on the floor and laying my head down on my pillow while the room spun around me. Though I didn't understand what parental negligence was as a preschooler, the more freedom I had the more I began to sense that my life wasn't normal. Unfortunately, the circumstances never changed.

When the party wasn't at our house, my mom often took us to her boyfriend's place where the two of them would party and do unspeakable things while Wendy and I wandered freely. We often played in the grass out back where there was a pool.

One day I wandered out the sliding glass door toward a large beach ball that had caught my attention. It was floating near the pool's edge. I hurried over to the clear blue water, crouched down and stretched my arms out to retrieve it. But instead of pulling the ball toward me I lost my balance, fell on top of the ball and then into the water. Not yet knowing how to swim, I immediately sank to the bottom where I began gasping, surprised to find that instead of air, water was pouring into my lungs. My eyes widened and my body convulsed as I sucked in more and more water and began to drown. Then suddenly I blacked out.

Wendy happened to be looking out the sliding glass door at precisely the moment I fell into the pool. She ran to the pool's edge and peered into the water to discover my lifeless body on the bottom. She didn't know how to swim either, but she immediately ran to the nearby stairs and lowered her small body into the shallow end. With her head tilted back and face just above the water's surface, she shuffled to my body where she took a big breath and plunged her head into the water. Keeping her eyes open she reached down and grabbed my waistband with both hands. She dragged my limp body through the water and then tugged me up the steps and onto the cement deck where she laid me on my back. My lips were blue. My abdomen was not moving.

Wendy began pounding on my chest with both hands. She pounded over and over and over. She couldn't have known how grave the situation was but she knew her baby brother didn't look right. She kept pounding and pounding until, finally, water began to gush from my mouth and I started choking for air.

Color returned to my lips as oxygen resurrected my lifeless body.

•••

Most children can run to mommy or daddy when they have a nightmare experience like that. But what are you supposed to do when your mom is the cause of the nightmare and she's all you have?

I would eventually figure out that I could not put my hope in my mom. It was a devastating revelation—realizing that the woman who brought me into the world, the woman I lived with and depended on and who I could not stop loving even if I tried, was one of the greatest enemies of my dreams. Sadly, it would take several years and many more nightmare experiences before I finally understood that truth of my circumstances.

One of the most vivid experiences took place when I was in first grade and shared a bed on the cement floor of our basement with Wendy. One night she and I were startled awake at two o'clock in the morning. My mom was having withdrawals and needed a fix. She yanked back our covers, grabbed our arms and dragged us up the basement stairs. Still wearing our pajamas, she took us out the side door of our house into the cold, and shoved us into the backseat of our rusted-out, blue Ford Escort. We weren't wearing seatbelts. There was no booster seat. Wendy and I were on the floorboard of the backseat, wiping the sleep from our eyes and trying to figure out what was going on. The engine sputtered to life, and we screeched from the curb and accelerated into the darkness.

I watched the asphalt whipping by beneath us. When I peaked out the side window I could see that we were heading into a dirty area of town—even dirtier than where we lived. We passed beat-up cars along crumbling curbs and dilapidated houses with dirt yards littered with trash. I didn't know it at the time but my mom was taking us to what they called "laboratories." Today they call them crack houses. It wouldn't be the only time we paid them a visit.

On some nights, my mom would leave us locked in the car while she went inside. Other times she locked us in the trunk. In her messed-up state of mind, she thought we would be safest there. This particular night she screeched to a halt next to a busted-out street lamp and barked at us to get out of the car. The second we stepped onto the sidewalk, she yanked us up a decaying staircase and into a rundown, two-story Victorian house.

A smoky haze floated out as my mom opened the front door. We stepped inside. The house was quiet and dark. A few drug addicts were passed out on the floor with haphazard piles of garbage around them. The only light inside originated from the moon reaching through the broken windows and soiled curtains. There was no furniture, no lamps or beds except for a dirty mattress in one corner. My mom pulled us down a hallway that led to the back of the house. I remember the sounds of our footsteps on the creaky floorboards. My eyelids had been heavy in the car, but now they were wide open. My heart was racing with fear.

We passed a man slumped against the wall just before reaching an old wooden door. Only a few strips of white paint still clung to it. The hinge creaked as my mom slowly pulled the door open.

The room was cold and the air was grayed with cigarette smoke. You could barely make out a door at the opposite end. As soon as we stepped inside, my mom pressed Wendy and me to the floor and motioned for us to stay put. Without a word she continued alone toward the other door. Wendy and I crawled into the nearest corner.

I remember feeling Wendy's body trembling as she pulled me close. Her long brown hair brushed against my cheek as our eyes adjusted to the dim, smoky light. That's when we noticed the longhaired man sitting guard by the other door. He admitted my mom to pass and then turned his gaze in our direction. His face was sharp and he wore leather boots, skintight jeans and a tie-dyed shirt. Against his chin he held the short barrel of a silver handgun. His eyes remained fixed on us. They didn't blink.

Wendy brought her quivering lips to my ear and told me to stay still and quiet and that everything would be okay. I tried not to move a single muscle and I kept my eyes closed like Wendy taught me.

Quietly and as still as two children could be, we spent the next hour pressed together, praying that mom would come out of that room and take us home. Compared to that place, our old, rundown apartment seemed like heaven.

We waited. And waited. And waited. Our little bodies were exhausted but fear of the staring man kept us awake.

Finally, the door behind him creaked and opened slowly. My mom walked through. Having had her fix, she was smiling and seemed happy. I jumped up and ran to her side, hugging one of her legs, She led us out of the house, put us back in the car and drove us home. Once we were inside the house, she instructed us to go back to bed.

Wendy and I hurried down the basement stairs to our bedroom where we immediately climbed back under the covers. My sister then rubbed my forehead and sang songs to me. I'll never forget watching her reach over my body and setting the alarm clock to make sure we'd wake up for school.

Two hours later, the alarm sounded and Wendy helped me out of bed. At her instruction, I slid into the same clothes I'd worn the day before. Wendy then looked me over and sent me to the mirror to fix my bed head. I took a look at myself and did my best to brush my hair down so I wouldn't get made fun of at school. Then we headed upstairs and checked on our mom. When we realized she was still passed out, we walked to the kitchen where we fixed our own cereal and packed our backpacks before heading out the front door.

As we left the house, Wendy turned the lock on the doorknob to make sure our mom would be safe while we were away. Then we walked to the bus stop where we stood with the other kids in the neighborhood and tried to act like everything was fine.

But everything wasn't fine.

My mom's choices continually put us in harm's way. As she fell deeper into addiction, the consequences escalated for us all. They also became more personal.

3

THE LOWEST OF LOWS

THE LOWEST OF LOWS

When my mom, Wendy and I left a convenience store one afternoon, we didn't know she was high and about to snap. I had to hurry to keep up as she marched across the parking lot to our car. I climbed into the front seat and Wendy climbed into the back.

The moment we pulled out of the parking lot, my mom floored the accelerator and began screaming, "You don't love me!" We quickly reached thirty, then forty, then fifty miles per hour on the crowded city streets. She weaved the car in and out of traffic. When we came to a clearing, she swung her door open and turned her legs like she was going to jump. "Everything will be better if I'm dead!" she yelled.

"Stop!" I screamed, and lunged to grab her shirt.

Her body whipped around and she backhanded me across the face. Blood began to pour from a deep split in my lip. Just then she spotted a police car. She whipped the car down a back road and pulled into a random driveway. She pushed me down to the floorboard and commanded us to stay down and hide. I tucked myself beneath the dash, pressing my hand to my lip, bleeding and crying, as she hissed warnings about the danger of the police finding us. She would go to prison, she insisted, and we would be taken away to live with someone we didn't know.

We sat idling in that driveway for what must have been twenty minutes, enough time for my mom to calm down. That's when she noticed my lip. It was busted open and bleeding badly. She hurried us home and patched up my lip. Then we carried on with life as if nothing had happened.

Moments like those caused confusing emotions in me—then, and years later as a teenager—because after she'd hurt me, my mom was, if only for a short time, caring and compassionate. In a sickening way, I sometimes felt as though the abuse was worth the remorseful love she showed afterward. Often it was the only time she conveyed something other than disappointment, annoyance or abandonment. In a surprising way, those brief moments of peace and affection were also small lights of hope in the dark tunnel of our existence, for all of us—but especially my dad.

Somehow, he remained hopeful that my mom could overcome the odds and rise above her addictions even after they were divorced. But he couldn't ignore the fact that my mom's selfish choices were becoming more and more perilous for Wendy and me. My mom hid most of the horrors of our life from my dad while she had custody, but after she went on a partying binge and abandoned us at home for three days, my dad finally convinced her to relinquish custody to him. Unfortunately, it turned out to be only a temporary relief.

My dad was soon laid off from his job at the Ford Motor Company during a time when jobs were difficult to find, especially in the auto industry. Unable to land another full-time job, he was forced to take one temporary part-time job after another, often working two and three jobs at a time to make ends meet. It eventually caught up to him.

When he couldn't afford to pay our rent, he had no choice but to move us back into our grandmother's house. My mom was living just down the street at the time, which allowed us to see her on a regular basis and allowed my dad to continue trying to help her. But it also kept us close to the chaos that always surrounded her; and she had been using drugs heavily again.

One night shortly after we moved in with our grandmother, Wendy and I were visiting my mom. The three of us were sitting on her bed watching TV when Wendy stood to retrieve something from across the room, leaving my mom and me sitting cross-legged on the knotted bedspread. I looked up at my mom with a smile, and that's when I noticed her face was blank and she was staring straight ahead. Her lips were trembling. She didn't glance back at me. Instead she reached into her nightstand drawer and grabbed a spoon and a plastic bag. She then pulled a lighter from the pocket of her faded jeans. Her hand quivering, she placed a small, white rock from the plastic bag onto the spoon and then flicked the lighter. She held the shaking spoon in front of her and raised the flame until it touched its underside. I watched the white rock begin to sizzle.

When Wendy realized what was happening, she jumped back onto the bed.

"Mom, please!" she pleaded. "Don't!"

As if in slow motion, I watched the mattress give way to Wendy's weight and then come back with a jolt, startling my mom from her trance. Then I watched as tiny beads of liquid cocaine rolled from the spoon's edge and tumbled to the bedspread.

My mom closed the lighter into her fist and backhanded Wendy in the mouth. Wendy tumbled to the floor whimpering as blood began to drip from where a tooth had pierced her bottom lip.

"Mom!" I screamed. "Don't do this! Stop!"

She shoved me off the bed and then reached down to my waistband. With one yank, she ripped the belt from my pants. I could see the track marks on her arm. I scooted close to Wendy while our mom heated another piece of rock and drew the liquid into a syringe.

Pulling my belt tight around her upper arm, she knotted it firmly and then located a vein. She stabbed the needle into her flesh and pushed the hot liquid into her arm.

We knew what normally came next, but this time was different. Instead of lying back in zombie-like state, Wendy and I watched in horror as our mom's eyes rolled back in her head and she fell off the bed and onto the hardwood floor with a terrible thud.

We scurried to her side and began shaking her body.

"Mom! Mom! Are you okay?"

Her eyelids were shut. Her arms were limp. Her chest was not moving.

I was too young to comprehend what was happening, but the panic in Wendy's voice made my heart start racing.

"Pound on her chest, Chad!" she ordered. "And don't stop!"

She ran into the kitchen to call our grandmother who immediately dialed 9-1-1. The paramedics were housed just down the street and within minutes, medical personnel and police officers flooded into the house.

Someone scooped up Wendy and carried her away, wiping the blood and tears from her face. An officer took my arm and led me to a corner of the bedroom. He knelt down in front of me and began asking me questions. I stretched my neck around him to see my mom's face so that I would know when she opened her eyes. The officer gently took my face into his rough hands and turned it toward him as he continued talking. I heard his voice but understood nothing he said as my ears were suddenly attuned to a male paramedic's words.

"She's unresponsive," he proclaimed. "There's no pulse."

The two men kneeling over her began administering CPR.

The officer immediately swept me out of the room

and down the hallway. As we left the doorway, I stretched my neck one last time hoping to see her wake up. I didn't. My last image was of a kneeling paramedic pressing on her chest over and over and over.

I felt my own my chest pounding as if my heart was going to burst through my ribcage. I knew I was losing my mom. Despite all she had done, despite all the pain and rejection and abandonment, I still loved her.

I didn't want to lose her.

No sooner had these thoughts passed through my head than I heard: "She's gone."

I stopped breathing.

My body went numb.

Everything in my head went silent.

Despite the valiant efforts of the paramedics, she hadn't responded.

The cocaine had stopped her heart.

She was dead.

When the officer heard the paramedic's words, he stood and began to lead me to another room further away.

That's when we both heard another voice.

"We've got a pulse!"

Everything jumped into overdrive. The volume in the room shot to full blast. I could hear every footstep, every voice, every beep and click of the medical equipment. The paramedics loaded my mom onto a gurney and rushed her down the hallway past us. Within minutes the men closed the back doors of the ambulance and sped to the hospital where my mom would make a full recovery.

•••

Two days later, I was back in my assigned seat in school, singing songs and learning my ABC's. A few weeks later my dad took my mom back in to live with us. It seemed she had learned her lesson and, as a result, the whole family was on the road to full recovery. Our house was peaceful for the first time that I could remember in my childhood. But a few weeks later, while riding home from the store in our car, it became clear the peace was temporary.

My dad was driving. My mom was in the passenger seat. Wendy and I were in the backseat, unaware that she had fallen back into her old ways and was strung out.

Out of nowhere my mom grabbed the seatbelt and wrapped it around her neck.

"Look!" she yelled to us in the back. "Your dad is choking me!"

We could see she was doing it herself and said so. She erupted in insults aimed at all three of us as we pulled into our driveway. As soon as my dad shifted into park, my mom yanked the keys from the ignition and then pressed her cigarette into my dad's leg, trying to pull him into a fight.

Wendy and I slid out of the car and watched through the window as my mom lifted the keys to her mouth and slashed them hard across her gums. Flying out of the front seat and pointing at her bloodstained teeth, she looked at Wendy and me and screamed, "Look! Look what your dad just did! He hit me! This is why I do what I do!"

"No, Mom," Wendy replied. "I saw what you did with the keys."

My mom snatched Wendy's arm and dragged her up the stairs of our duplex as she continued to scream insults. My dad and I ran after her to pull Wendy away. Once inside, my mom began flailing her open fists on my dad's face and body. He covered up and moved into the kitchen to avoid further conflict. My mom chased after him. From just outside the room, I watched as she grabbed dishes and glasses from the sink and began throwing them against the walls, floor and countertop. Ceramic and glass shards flew through the air with each crash. Then suddenly my mom scooped up a dining room chair and ran toward the second story window. She slammed the legs through the windowpane and then swung the chair against the window again and again until most of the glass was gone as well as the drywall around the frame.

My dad watched in shock as white dust clouded the area where the window once was. My mom then tossed the chair aside and began crawling through the opening, screaming over and over that we didn't love her and she wanted to die.

My dad rushed over and grabbed her arm.

"Let go of me!" she screamed.

Shaking, I watched as she pushed and kicked at my dad to free herself. Just then, Wendy gripped my shoulders and led me into the back bedroom. Shouts and screams filtered back to us as my dad tried to save my mom from herself. Wendy guided me to the floor where she sat next to me and, with silent tears rolling down her face, prayed that it all would stop.

4

LEARNING HOW TO HOPE

LEARNING HOW TO HOPE

My dad saved my mom from jumping that day, but he couldn't always be there to protect her, and us, from the choices she continued to make. From that day on, chaos was as regular in my home as dinner. As an elementary school kid, I could do nothing about it. I was still dependent on my parents to provide me with food, clothes and a roof over my head. Unfortunately, that dependence came with a steep price.

As I grew older, we seemed to move with increasing frequency. My dad's job situation never stabilized for long and that meant two things: I had to attend a new school about every six months, and Wendy and I remained vulnerable to the consequences of my mom's addictions.

Being in school and under the primary care of my dad kept Wendy and me from some harm, but not all of it. His temporary work and multiple jobs kept him away often and my mom couldn't help but bring her violent, chaotic life to us.

The physical horrors that I witnessed were terrifying and kept me up many nights as a child. But, in hindsight, the emotional destruction of my mom's choices was worse.

Hope is an interesting word. While it is a critical part of thriving in life, it can also be a killer if your hope is in the wrong things. When I was young, I didn't know how not to put my hope in my mom. I didn't fully comprehend that she was choosing to feed her addictions over my and Wendy's well-being, again and again. I didn't understand that while she wasn't killing me in the physical sense, her choices repeatedly put me on death's doorstep. I didn't know that wanting to feel her love, support and approval was foolish, given her history. But as I grew older, I began to understand.

I remember the day when I realized I hadn't known more than a few weeks of normalcy in my entire life. I was ten years old, and the realization hit me like a punch in the gut. It was as if someone opened the door to a new world and suddenly, I began to notice how other families looked and how other moms treated their kids and how other kids talked about their parents. I suddenly saw in clear detail how very different I was from every other kid in my class.

Their lives were peaceful and perfect. My life was dominated by terror and tragedy. Between my mom's issues and my dad's struggles with depression and unemployment, I was the furthest thing from a normal kid.

To make matters worse, we had already moved nearly a dozen times. The instability wore me thin. Loneliness began to creep in. I wanted more than anything to settle into one house in one location where I could make some friends and keep them, and where I could play on the same sports teams for more than one season. I often remember thinking that when I was old enough I was going to do whatever was needed to create stability for my future family.

For a brief season, it seemed that my wish was coming true, thanks in large part to my dad's unrelenting efforts to help my mom. She had left the family again, and then surprised us after a few weeks by showing up where we were living in Cincinnati, Ohio. As he always did, my dad took her back. The next year and a half represented the best season our family ever had together. Wendy and I built good friendships, my dad was holding down a good job and we lived in a decent home. My mom remained clean and was working too.

When she was free of her addictions, my mom was caring and involved in our lives. She helped us with our homework each afternoon, made us delicious meals every night and planned regular get-togethers with our new friends. When it came time to celebrate my eleventh birthday, she planned a big afternoon at the pizza place complete with all the games. Afterward, we would all head back to our house to eat some cake and ice cream, and then all the guys were going to spend the night. I was finally going to enjoy a normal birthday party like other kids.

When the school bell rang, my friends and I bolted for our house, joking and wrestling along the way. A few minutes later, we tumbled through the front door.

The silence immediately caught my attention. I looked around. The place was immaculate—a telltale sign that my mom had left us again. My heart sank.

"Hello, Birthday Boy!" Wendy exclaimed as she hopped into the room and snapped a cardboard birthday hat on my head.

I leaned close to her ear and whispered in near panic, "Where's Mom?"

"I don't know," she whispered back. "But don't worry. Dad will be home in plenty of time to get us to the pizza place. Relax." She nudged me into the living room where the guys had already started a video game tournament.

I couldn't relax until my dad came through the door ten minutes later. The sudden momentum of the party helped me forget about my mom for a few hours. But that night, after all the fun had ceased and my friends were all asleep on my bedroom floor, the tears of disappointment came. I lay there awake for an hour, silent tears rolling off my cheeks and onto my pillow. Then I heard the front door open. My heart began to pound.

I slid from my sleeping bag and vaulted over the bodies of my sleeping friends. Creeping down the stairs, I stopped at the living room entryway and peeked around the corner. My mom was sprawled out on the couch.

Everyone in the house was asleep, so I crept over to her and tried to think of a way to get her to bed quietly. I could smell the alcohol as I reached the couch, and I noticed a wad of money in her right hand.

"Hi, Mom," I said softly.

"Oh," she said, surprised. "Hi."

"Hey, Mom, where'd you get the money? Were you playing craps? Wow, you must have been really good to win all that!"

"What?" she said in a daze, her eyes still closed.

"Mom, I love you," I said, taking her by the hand and helping her up. "You must be tired. Come on, you should go to bed."

"No, I'm not tired at all," she replied in a louder voice.

"Come on, Mom," I said softly, placing her arm around my shoulder. "That's right."

I quietly led her up the stairs and helped her into bed next to my dad without waking him up. I then returned to my room and wove my way through my friends' sleeping bags until I reached mine. I pulled it open and slid back inside. It was still warm.

As I lay there, I felt crushed inside. The last year and a half had been the best time of my life. I truly believed that my mom had overcome her addictions. I thought things were finally going to be normal for our family. But once again my hope had been dashed. I knew her relapse wouldn't last just one night, and that it would probably begin another difficult period for my dad, sister and me.

I started thinking about my dad and how he must have felt, how hard this must have been on him. Then I thought about something he always told Wendy and me about the importance of having hope. "Hope will always keep you going," he'd emphasize. "No matter how bad things seem, and as long as your mom has breath there is still hope for her—don't ever give up on her."

I was beginning to learn the truth of those words. My dad was teaching us that there are two ways to see every circumstance. I could look at the disappointing facts of my life: my mom had left again, she was still addicted and it wasn't fair that I still suffered from her choices. Or I could look at the signs of hope: she had been clean for the longest period of time since I was born, she still had breath in her lungs and I had finally tasted a better life.

Even though I was disappointed about my mom missing my birthday—and even though I would be disappointed by her again—I finally understood that I could still hopebecause my hope was about my own choices, not hers. No matter what she did or how her choices affected my life, I still chose how I was going to view my circumstances and myself in light of them. My life was either doomed or it was destined to turn around. I could either sulk at my own private pity party or I could rise up and do all I could to turn things around. Simply put, I could quit or start to shape my own destiny.

On the night of my eleventh birthday, I learned that even though the world labeled me an at-risk kid, I could fight for the things I wanted in life. And even though my circumstances said I would amount to nothing more than a statistic, I had a hand in whether that proved to be true. It was the beginning of my informal education in chasing my dreams.

I had more ignorance than knowledge back then, but I made up for the deficit with a growing reservoir of grit and determination inside me. I would need every last bit of it as I transitioned into middle school where the kids no longer played nice if you didn't fit in. I would also need the grit and determination to deal with a new set of circumstances that my mom's addictions introduced.

When I was thirteen, I enrolled in my fourteenth new school, this time in North Carolina where my dad had taken another temporary job. My mom remained behind in Michigan to complete rehab. While I was tired of being the new kid, the constant change helped me grow a thick skin. I cared less and less about what people thought of me. To that point, I had been the chubby kid. But by the eighth grade, I was thinning out and rapidly growing into a man's body.

When I entered my new middle school in North Carolina, I was a little over six feet tall and nearly 200 pounds. Basketball was quickly becoming more than a game to me. Along with my size advantage, I was discovering I had some natural ability; namely, that I could jump like I had springs on my feet. When I dunked for the first time in a game that year, it ignited a full-blown passion inside me. I remember the feeling after the game, sitting in the locker room and replaying the dunk over and over in my mind. It was like a confirmation that I wasn't crazy thinking I could play in college and even professionally one day. All I wanted to do right then was get to a basketball court and dunk some more. Confidence began to build inside me, as well as a faith that this future I dreamed of could actually come true.

We didn't have a hoop at our place, so the moment my dad and I pulled into our driveway, I walked to the neighbor's house and asked if I could shoot on the basketball goal that was mounted to their garage. They gladly allowed me to and went so far to say that I could shoot anytime I wanted (little did they know that I would practically live in their driveway when I wasn't at school). I shot around and practiced dunks for the next couple of hours.

Over the days and weeks that followed, I played every chance I got—after practice, after games and for hours-on-end over the weekends. I was finally pursuing something that mattered to me and taking steps toward my dream. People had been telling me that playing Division I college basketball, let alone professional ball, was impossible for someone like me. I cared less and less about what they said. I kept playing and kept fighting to improve. My hope was no longer bound up in what others thought, said or did. It was bound up in my own skill and will.

5

FIGHTING THE RIGHT FIGHT

FIGHTING THE RIGHT FIGHT

During that same season, I also began taking a stand for my mom who had completed rehab and was totally clean by the time my dad and I moved back to Detroit. Something had switched inside me. Now, instead of simply trying to defend myself from the circumstances of my life, I was on the offensive on all fronts. I was asserting my strengths into my circumstances and trying to change them for the better.

Once back in Detroit, I moved in with my mom because my dad was again out of work and battling depression. My mom had a steady job that provided health insurance. She also lived near the high school I would attend. Unfortunately, all was not as peaceful as I planned.

While my mom managed to remain off drugs and alcohol, she made horrible decisions about the guys she dated and eventually allowed to live in our house. The very thing that helped her get clean became the catalyst for a new kind of chaos.

Among addicts, there is no shortage of violent men, and my mom's boyfriends had all the tendencies. Most of them she befriended through rehab or her ongoing participation in Alcoholics Anonymous. Strong, addictive personalities are a volatile combination and, left unchecked, these so-called boyfriends eventually turned violent.

Physical violence quickly became the backdrop of my ninth grade year. Every night there seemed to be some sort of altercation. One night my mom came home with a broken leg from where her boyfriend had jumped on her repeatedly. On another night I watched her boyfriend smash her head into the windshield of her red Pontiac. Once again, I hadn't chosen the circumstances. But now I was done watching from the sidelines.

I had grown even taller and stronger by this point and, while I was still a mere fourteen years old, I had a lifetime's worth of turmoil built up inside me. Eventually it started boiling out in defense of my mom.

For a while, fighting my mom's boyfriends seemed to be the one thing I was more talented at than basketball. I didn't always win, but I usually held my own and I always left each boyfriend with enough cuts and bruises to give him something to think about the next time he tried to hurt my mom on my watch.

The good news is that my classmates no longer made fun of me for wanting to play college and professional basketball, especially as I continued to grow bigger and taller. Instead they would make fun of me for not having the best clothes or shoes.

I was still the kid that would come to school two or three days in row wearing the same clothes—the same shirt, the same jeans, day after day. The cool kids would even make fun of me because my socks didn't match.

I remember sitting in homeroom, looking at these kids who thought they had it all together and thinking to myself, *Man, if these kids only knew what I had been through last night—if they could have just been in my house and seen my mom come stumbling in the front door with her bottom row of teeth knocked flat in her mouth and her boyfriend thumping her in the back of the head—they wouldn't be making fun of me right now.*

What my classmates didn't know was that my appearance didn't tell the whole story. They thought I was just lazy or messy, or both. What they didn't know was that I was up until four in the morning, fighting my mom's boyfriend, trying to defend her from another bloodied face and another broken bone. Sure, I got to school the next day and my socks didn't match, but that's because I ran out of the house that morning having slept two hours, slipping one sock on at a time, to the sound of my mom's boyfriend cussing me out all the way to school. What the cool kids didn't know was that I didn't sleep a lot of nights because I was up brawling with grown men until the break of dawn.

While defending my mom might sound heroic or glamorous, it was exactly the opposite. Eventually it took its toll. The constant violence tore me down on the inside. It was as though my mom's demons had seen my passion and confidence increase and they decided to come at me with everything they had.

On one fateful night, I had just walked home from basketball practice, hoping to relax on the couch and recover from my exhaustion. When I pushed open our front door, two faces turned toward me in surprise.

My eyes adjusted to the dim light of the living room as the door slammed hard against the frame behind me. Frozen and staring at me were my mom and her boyfriend. His left forearm was forcing her body against the living room wall, while the other arm was drawn back in a clenched fist. Time seemed to pause for a few seconds as each of us took in the scene.

Then everything accelerated.

Once he realized it was just me at the door, he smirked and then slammed his fist into my mom's face. Blood began to pour from her mouth as her body crumpled to the floor. I threw the bag off my shoulder and rushed at him, landing a right hook on his jaw. He staggered but didn't fall. He returned a right uppercut deep into my gut and I dropped to my knees, breathless but not deterred. I lunged at his legs, picked him up and threw him to the floor. From my knees I snatched a nearby lamp and smashed it against the side of his head. I stood back up and began moving toward my mom, thinking the fight was over.

It wasn't.

The boyfriend shot up and rushed me. Before I could defend myself he kicked me in my right shin with his steel-toe boots. I dropped to the ground writhing in pain, and he immediately jumped on top of me and started punching me. I covered my face because I didn't want marks to have to explain at school the next day. He started pounding me, again and again, in my abdomen. Eventually, the blows cracked two of my ribs. I couldn't breathe. As I dropped my hands to reposition myself, he punched me several times in the face. He didn't beat me up as bad as he could have, but he had his fill. He then wrapped his arms around me, lifted me up and dragged me to the back bedroom where he tossed me on the bed, cussing me out and swearing death over me if I tried anything else. He stormed out of the room and slammed the door behind him.

I rolled onto my side, gasping for air. My fists were still clenched as I studied the door, waiting for him to burst back through. It was how these fights typically went—one furious brawl after another until the cops showed up or the sun started to light the night.

The boyfriend didn't return that night, and I was left alone with my heart pounding and my face dripping blood and tears. I slowly licked the cut on my lower lip as I tried again to draw a deep breath.

"What's the point?" I exhaled.

There I was, barely a teenager, having to fight day in and day out with my mom's grown boyfriends when I should have been enjoying life with friends like a normal kid my age. Speaking of normal...I had barely known a normal day in my life. Was normalcy so much to ask for? After fourteen years of living among filthy people, violence and abuse, having to learn to protect myself from my own mom's choices, the weight of my circumstances finally crashed down on me.

My heart began crying out, over and over: *Why does life have to be so hard? Why does this have to keep happening to me? What did I do to deserve this?*

I reached a breaking point.

I began sobbing into my covers. "I can't do this anymore," I whispered. "No one cares. No one has ever cared. Who would even miss me if I was gone?"

I bit down on my bottom lip and felt the sharp sting from a cut. The first thought that ran through my mind was that I was probably busted up pretty bad. *What am I going to tell my teachers tomorrow at school?* I sat up on the edge of my bed, and then gingerly stood and looked in the mirror that was attached to a dresser. What I saw in my reflection is what I had grown accustomed to seeing. My right eye was nearly swollen shut. My lip was split open and a stream of blood was running down my chin and neck. My cut-off white t-shirt from practice was completely stretched out and I had large purple and red scratch marks all over my upper body. This wasn't just a breaking point for me—I was done.

I was finally facing the toughest fight every single one of us faces—the fight within ourselves. At fourteen years old, I wasn't simply fighting against poverty or my mom's abusive boyfriends or my schoolmates' ridicule, and I knew it. Underneath it all, I was fighting for things like peace, normalcy and, most of all, purpose. I desperately wanted to believe my life had a greater meaning than survival—that my life could really look like I had hoped it would since I was a small boy. I wanted to thrive, but as I lay there in my bed after yet another violent brawl, it seemed foolish to believe it was even possible. I wasn't sure I could muster the strength to fight again. Part of me didn't even want to. I had inherited circumstances that seemed to constantly shove me in the opposite direction of the dreams I held inside. I wondered if the circumstances were telling me a truth I hadn't yet accepted—that I was bound to be surrounded by addiction, violence and pain for the rest of my life. *If that is my fate*, I thought, *what's the point in fighting against it*?

It was hard to see another future before me as a fourteen-year-old who'd been bruised and bloodied for what seemed like the thousandth time. I had risen to the challenge time and again—no one could say I hadn't tried to overcome it all—but now I was tired of fighting. I wanted out and quitting seemed to be the easiest way. I definitely knew it would be easier than rising up again.

Inside, I knew I only had two options. I could wipe off the blood and tears again and keep fighting for my dreams, even if the battles continued. Or I could surrender to my circumstances and let them dictate my future.

It was ultimately a decision about my potential. And most importantly, it was my decision. I was either going to let my circumstances place a ceiling on my potential or I was going to bust through that ceiling and rise as high as I possibly could.

Before I made a choice, I collapsed back on my bed and played a movie reel of memories in my mind. I saw the drugs, alcohol and unspeakable details of the parties in our living room. I heard the laughter of my mom's friends as I sipped the spiked Kool-Aid. I felt the nausea after my mom scooped the beer suds into my mouth. I felt the cold chills of the crack houses and the fright of the staring man with the gun. I watched my mom heat the drugs and shove them into her arm. I relived her chaotic overdose. I pictured every room I'd called my bedroom since I could remember. And then I relived the fights—the abuse and injuries I'd witnessed and the brawls I'd chosen to enter. It wasn't fair. It was far too much for any kid to bear.

I reached up and gently touched my right eye. It was now swollen shut. I licked my lip and tasted the dried blood. I grabbed a wad of my pillowcase and dabbed the tears from my cheeks and the corners of my eyes. I then took a deep breath and saw something I'd never seen before.

I saw that I was not the only one suffering in my story. And I was not the only one in my family fighting for his dreams.

I pictured my dad, who despite his struggles with depression and unemployment over the years, had never once given up. He'd humbled himself time and again, even to the point of moving back in with his own mother, as a full-grown adult with his own children, in order to make ends meet. He had been fighting for Wendy and me since we were babies. He'd been working two and three jobs for most of my life in order to provide food and clothes and a house for us. He fought for us in court to protect us from our mom's choices. He'd even been fighting for my mom since the day they met, even after she turned her back on him time and again. I realized he was still fighting that very night.

I pictured Wendy, who had suffered through just as much as I had—if not more—and yet she still managed to remain a consistently strong, faith-filled person. She'd been my guardian angel on more occasions than I could count, protecting me from the worst emotional and physical harm when I was too small to protect myself. She too had never stopped fighting, for herself or for me.

And then there was my mom. Despite the pain she'd caused me—and all of us—and despite the years' worth of selfish choices that made my childhood a never-ending nightmare, she had never stopped fighting. Even that night as she lay beaten and bleeding on the living room floor, she had gotten herself clean again through rehab. She was attending AA on a regular basis. She was holding down a good job and making a real effort to be a good mom. While she still was prone to terrible choices, and even though she could never undo the damage of her past, she was still fighting for her future. And now she was fighting for mine.

I realized that if my dad, Wendy and my mom could still find the strength to fight, I could too. I had no excuses. Closing my eyes, I made a personal vow that night to never let quitting be an option again. If somebody stole my life that was one thing; but I wasn't going to surrender it on my own.

I woke up the next morning and I cleaned the stains from my hands, face and neck. Then I left for school with a newfound conviction to chase my dreams no matter the cost. I knew the price would be high. I would have to learn just how high.

6

CLOSING IN ON MY DREAMS

CLOSING IN ON MY DREAMS

The following season, my sophomore year, I averaged over twenty points a game while my mom worked hard to slay her alcoholism for good. She became one of the biggest advocates of my dream to play college basketball. The following year, she and I made the decision that I would transfer to Detroit Catholic Central High School, which was on the radar of every college coach in America. It was also the seventeenth school I had attended since kindergarten.

The transfer to one of the top schools in the state was important, but it also introduced a new battle. I was the new kid, a complete unknown who hadn't grown up playing AAU basketball with the other kids on the team. I was transferring in as a junior, and I had already moved around too much for any colleges to know who I was. I had to prove myself right away, and the only way to do that was to let my game speak for itself.

By season's end, I averaged twenty-four points and twelve rebounds a game. College coaches from all over the country began to take notice. It helped that by this point I had nearly grown into my full 6' 7" frame.

Basketball became more than an escape. Through the sport I began to unpack my purpose and mature into a man. The process involved learning lessons I hadn't been taught growing up.

My Hall of Fame coach, Bernie Holowicki, introduced me to the principles of discipline and dedication. I began to understand the level of focus and hard work necessary to make my dreams a reality. He always told me that it wasn't enough to be talented and believe that I could make it. I had to put in the work to continually improve my game, he insisted, and all that hard work would eventually open the doors that would lead to greater opportunities for me. While I had size and was blessed with the ability to jump out of the gym, I had to turn those raw advantages into becoming an all-around player when it really mattered during a game. Coach Holowicki helped me see that there was so much more to being a great basketball player than just being an athlete who was able to pull off acrobatic dunks. He taught me that if I was going to realize my dreams, I had to give more to basketball than anything else—even more than having fun with my friends.

One particular night epitomized my perspective. I had one of the best games of my life. I scored fifty-seven points, including nine dunks, and I was hitting three-pointers from everywhere. High-fives and hollers filled the locker room after the game. Coach congratulated us on the win and told us that he was giving us the next day off from practice. As soon as he said we didn't have practice the next day, some of the guys on my team started smiling and nudging each other. I knew what they were thinking. They could go out and party and not have to worry about being hung over the next day at practice.

After we put our hands in the huddle and said our little "Hoo-Rah," I took a shower, got dressed and grabbed my bag to head out of the locker room.

"Hey, Chad," one of my teammates called. "Great game, man!"

"Why don't you come hang out, come party with us tonight?" another yelled.

"Nah, I don't think so," I called back, turning toward my locker.

"Why not?" he continued. "You just had the one of the best games of your life. It's time to celebrate!"

"Thanks guys, but I don't think so."

"Come on, Chad," one of the others petitioned. "You don't have to get drunk, man. Just come hang out with us. You deserve it."

I stared at my locker. "Nah, I have some work to do, guys."

And that's when they started throwing their verbal jabs at me.

"What are you, soft?"

"You can't hang?"

"What's the deal with you?"

They didn't like my answer and I didn't like disappointing them. But at the end of the day, I had learned what I needed to do and what I had to give up in order to pursue my dreams.

I quickly made my way out of the locker room and was met by my dad. He was all smiles. He threw his arm around my shoulder. "That's my boy!" he repeated. I stopped to sign a couple of autographs for some elementary school kids when one of my teammates slid by me in the crowded hallway and shoved his thumb into my ribs.

"You should be partying with us, man," he whispered, "not going home with your old man. What's wrong with you?"

I was glad when my dad and I finally reached the car. I slid inside and quickly shut the door, finally silencing all the jeers of my friends and teammates who didn't understand what I was doing.

The irony is that my buddies always said the same things I said. They talked about how they were going to play college and pro ball one day. However, that night while they were popping tops and sucking suds, talking to the girls about how they were "the man," I was doing something entirely different. While my teammates were hanging out talking about their dreams, I was working toward mine.

I had barely begun, I told myself. But I was on my way.

At the end of my junior season, I was invited to Ohio to play against one hundred of the best high school basketball players in the Midwest for a chance to earn one of ten spots on the Midwest All-Star team. If I made the team we would be going on to play at the Las Vegas Invitational tournament in Nevada. This was a huge opportunity for me to be seen, because just about every college coach in America would be there, recruiting.

I dominated on the first morning of the tournament. When they posted the player cuts, I had made it into the top twenty. In high spirits, I walked back to my room to rest before the late evening session.

As I prepared to take an afternoon nap, I removed the contact from my left eye and it tore. I stared down in disbelief at the small disc on the tip of my finger. I couldn't see without it.

I found a pay phone and called home to Michigan. Wendy answered and I told her about the contact.

"Oh, no!" she exclaimed. "You are practically blind without them. How are you going to play?"

"I don't know. Is dad home?"

"No, he's still at work."

"Wendy, I really can't see without my contact. I don't know how I can possibly play like this."

"Well, you'll just have to suck it up and do your best."

"Yeah, you're right," I said, unable to hide my dejection.

I took a long walk after I hung up the phone. I tried not to think about the consequences of blowing this opportunity. I knew I had to persevere. Not playing didn't even cross my mind. But it was impossible to quell my anxiety.

Later that evening, I walked out of the training room

after having my ankles taped, prepared for what I thought was going to be the biggest challenge of my life—playing with one eye. I was no more than ten steps from the training room when an assistant coach approached me. He placed a small box in my hands.

"Someone just gave this to me to give to you," he said. "I think it was your dad. Does he drive a little Ford Escort?"

"Yeah," I said, opening the box.

I pulled out a note, written in my dad's familiar handwriting. "Chad, I love you," he wrote. "Here's a contact—do your best, Son. I'm proud of you. I know you can do it!"

I let out a whoop and ran back into the locker room to put in the contact. Then I jogged back out on the court with renewed confidence.

Afterward, I called Wendy from the same pay phone.

"Hey, Wen! I got the contact! And I'm going to Las Vegas!"

"I called dad at the plant after I got off the phone with you," she explained. "When he asked about leaving to get you a contact, his boss gave him a hard time. The only way they agreed to let him go was if he worked a double-shift as soon as he got back."

"Where'd he get the money for the contact?"

"I don't know, Chad. He must have borrowed it. But he's going to be really glad to hear you made the team."

"Tell him he's the best dad in the world and I love him!"

I hung up the phone and pulled the note out of my

pocket to read it again. My dad had modeled heroism before, most notably with his efforts to save my mom. He seemed to always come through when given the chance. But he weaved another more prominent thread in my life that would eventually find its way into my heart too. He was my hero for certain; but more than that, he was a servant. I would eventually understand what that meant. That knowledge would change everything.

I played some of the best basketball of my life that week in Las Vegas, making the all-tournament team and leaving as one of the top recruits in the country. My senior year I averaged 28.3 points, 14 rebounds and 6 blocked shots per game. I was named first team all-league, all-Catholic, all-district, all-region and all-state. I was also nominated to the McDonald's All-American team. Soon, I was sorting through scholarship offers from colleges all across the nation.

• • •

"What about Florida State, Chad?" my dad asked, handing me their basketball program.

"I don't know," I said, running my hand through my hair.

My dad and I were sorting through the dozens of scholarship offers that had poured in from schools across the country. Some of them were highly touted basketball schools. It was the biggest decision of my life to that point. I wanted to make the right choice, and I was ready to leave the turmoil in Detroit behind. There were too many bad memories there and I was ready for a fresh start. While my dad and I did our due diligence, I didn't take long to pick a school and enroll early.

I chose the University of Richmond because I felt I could start as a freshman and I had a great relationship with the head coach, Dick Tarrant. He was one of the top coaches in the country, and he had led the Richmond program to unprecedented success in the NCAA Tournament by beating Indiana and Syracuse. Unfortunately, my plan didn't work out as I had intended.

Shortly into pre-season conditioning, I developed a season-ending stress fracture in my right foot. I was forced to sit out the entire season as a medical red-shirt. Then I learned that Coach Tarrant had decided to retire at the end of the season. I began considering other options. In the end, the primary reason I decided to play basketball at the University of Richmond was Coach Tarrant. With him leaving, I decided to transfer to another university.

I decided to transfer to a school in the Big Ten until I learned that NCAA rules required a player who transfers from one Division I school to another to sit out one complete year. If I followed that path, two years would pass without me having played competitive basketball.

That's when I learned that if I transferred to a junior college, I could play the very next season. I visited some of the best junior colleges in the nation and eventually decided to play at top-ranked Vincennes University in Indiana. Once I enrolled at Vincennes, Division I universities would have the opportunity to recruit me again.

Still, it was a junior college. That posed risks. First, it meant giving up my four-year scholarship at Richmond. If I was injured during the next season at Vincennes, I would never obtain another Division I scholarship. My basketball and academic dreams would likely be over.

I decided to take the risk and headed to Vincennes for what would be my red-shirt freshman year. Many people thought it was a foolish decision, but when I met the most beautiful girl in the world a few weeks into my first semester, I knew I'd made one of the best decisions of my life, basketball or no basketball.

At Vincennes my life entered a really good season— the best of my life to that point. My parents were supporting me from afar; I'd met Kristie, the love of my life, whom I would marry the next year; and I was tearing it up on the basketball court. I averaged 19.6 points and 9.4 rebounds per game. I was named a Junior College Division I All-American and had scholarship offers from just about every major Division I school.

Over the months that followed, Kristie and I sat in my dorm room and sifted through piles of recruiting letters from schools in the Big East, ACC, Big Ten, SEC, PAC 10 and Big 12 conferences. I eventually narrowed my choices down to Kansas, Wake Forest, Pittsburgh, Wisconsin and Missouri.

Then one day I reached into a box and pulled out a letter that didn't belong.

"What's this?" I said to Kristie, holding up a greeting card envelope. It was from my dad. "It's postmarked two months ago. It must have been mixed in with all this other mail and I missed it."

Smiling, I opened the envelope and read the card. Then I handed it to Kristie.

She read it aloud: "Dear Chad, I love you, Son. I'm proud of you. This is all I could do for you, but I love you and hope it helps."

I reached into the envelope and retrieved two $1 bills.

"This was probably his last two dollars that week," I said, with tears in my eyes.

"Your dad is incredible!" Kristie replied, picking up the two bills from the table.

"You know, that means more to me than any of these scholarship offers."

I meant it. In truth, those two dollars meant so much they inspired me to try even harder at the University of Pittsburgh, where I chose to play ball next. I finished my junior season at Pittsburgh as the team's leading scorer and rebounder in Big East Conference play after averaging 14.3 points and 6.9 rebounds per game. I was named MVP of the team, and that summer I was invited to play on Team America, a collegiate all-star team that traveled to Italy and played many of the foreign Olympic teams prior to them facing our Dream Team in the upcoming Olympic games.

Basketball had become my life and had allowed me to play with some of the greatest basketball players in the world. My dream was within reach. Coming into my senior season, expectations were high. Then, right before the start of the season, I fractured a bone above my right ankle.

While I was incredibly frustrated, I treated the injury like any other challenge. I did everything I could to heal as quickly as possible, and then played through the pain. When the season was over, I was invited as a free agent to play in the NBA with the Dallas Mavericks.

Then a broken hand just before training camp forced me to take a different path in my professional basketball career.

7

DISCOVERING MY BIGGER PURPOSE

DISCOVERING MY BIGGER PURPOSE

"How is it feeling?" Kristie asked as I sat next to her on the couch.

I looked at the cast on my hand.

"It's fine," I said. I reached over and gave her a hug.

I began sorting through the paperwork strewn across the coffee table. I explained to Kristie that with my broken hand, we were left with only two options. Either I could play in the CBA (Continental Basketball Association), which was like the minor leagues to the NBA, or I could play basketball in the European professional leagues.

"What do *you* think we should do?" Kristie asked.

"Look," I said, handing her several sheets of figures, "I've run the numbers over and over, and I think the only sensible thing both for my career and our financial future is to play in Europe."

"Where would we go?" Kristie asked.

I smiled. "How about Spain?

• • •

There are many wonderful parts of Europe, but Spain is particularly beautiful. Once my agent confirmed that one of the country's professional teams wanted to sign me, we made the move to a northern coastal city called Gijón. While I was working hard and excelling at my game, it felt a little like a full-time vacation. I wasn't making millions of dollars, but I was making more money than I had ever imagined. To make matters even better, we were provided with a beautiful home on the Bay of Biscay and a vehicle as part of my contract. Best of all, Kristie and I enjoyed the quality time we had together with our young son, Cameron, and our daughter, Kiersten, who was born that year in Spain.

My skills grew stronger each week of that rookie year. I was named player of the week four times, voted to start the All-Star game and won the slam-dunk contest. In my second season, we moved to Tenerife, Spain, located in the Canary Islands, known as the "Hawaii of Europe." We had an incredible team and an incredible year, ending league play as one of the top seeds heading into the playoffs. I was the team's leading scorer and rebounder, and was named an All-Star for the second consecutive season. I was also invited to play in a prestigious Nike summer league in Travieso, Italy. I had bounced back from my broken hand and, after a brief delay, had my future in basketball lined up before me. I was moving into my contract year, and my agent was negotiating offers bigger than I had ever seen.

As my final season in Tenerife was coming to an end and we were anticipating returning to our off-season home near Kristie's family, I had one of the best games of my professional career. I scored 36 points and pulled down 18 rebounds. After the game, Kristie, the kids and I drove to a restaurant with my agent to celebrate.

After winding down over a good meal, Kristie and I stood behind my agent's chair and reviewed all the offers that had come in from professional teams around Europe, including an invitation from the Chicago Bulls to join their training camp and a endorsement deal with Reebok. I'd worked so hard and overcome so much, and now it was time to cash in. I pulled Kristie next to me and we reveled in the possibilities before us.

As we drove home that night, I was still basking in the realization that I had finally made it. I'd finally be able to do the things I always dreamed about. I glanced at Kristie in the seat next to me and thought about everything we'd been through together, everything she'd endured since she became a part of my broken-down life. I glanced in the rearview mirror and I could see Cameron and Kiersten nodding off to sleep. Tears welled up in my eyes as I thought about being able to provide a life for them that I never had.

We arrived home, and Kristie and I scooped up the kids and tucked them into bed. Kristie hit the sack shortly thereafter. Still buzzing with emotion, I relaxed on the couch for a few minutes to wind down. Eventually my exhaustion caught up to me and I checked on Cameron and Kiersten before climbing into bed next to Kristie. I was out in minutes.

Around 2:30 a.m., something woke me up. It wasn't the phone or a bang on the door or even a sound from outside the window. It was like a sixth sense, a sound from deep inside me. I didn't want to wake Kristie, so I slid quietly out of bed and walked to the living room. I flipped on the light to our balcony and stepped outside.

As I stood in the cool night air, gazing over the Atlantic Ocean, my entire life began flashing before my eyes like a fast-paced slideshow. I saw everything I'd ever done since I was a child, and everything I was about to do. When the slideshow was finished, something I didn't expect came over me—a tangible, undeniable void.

I was on the verge of having everything I'd ever dreamed of and more. I was about to check off the final box on my dream list. College graduate? Check. Beautiful family? Check. Career in professional basketball? Check. Contract that would provide financial security for many years to come? Check.

I had achieved it all, but I couldn't ignore a feeling that something was still missing.

As I watched the moon's reflection flickering on the ocean waves, I reflected on my future beyond my dreams. One day, I admitted, my life would be over and the days between now and then would define me. People would say: "Chad Varga was born into a hard life. He overcame it by becoming a great basketball player. Then he died."

When my life was put like that it seemed so trite. I

asked myself, "Am I okay with that epitaph?"

I couldn't deny that I wanted more for my life than dunking a basketball or shooting a good jump shot. Was my highest potential really defined by playing basketball, living in a nice house and going to Disneyland with my family in the off-season?

One voice in my head shot back, "Yes! That's exactly what it's about, baby!"

But another voice wasn't buying it.

A debate ensued in my head.

Yes, I had managed to make myself into something despite nearly impossible odds. Yes, basketball was a huge part of that, and yes, I was a 6' 7" man with a 41-inch vertical jump. A career in basketball made perfect sense. But, while basketball had helped me get out of a broken home, the truth was that the memories and lessons learned in that broken home hadn't gotten out of me.

I couldn't help thinking about all the other kids living in places like where I grew up who would never find a way to escape their circumstances. Every time I watched the news I saw stories of shootings in schools, gang fights, teen suicide, drug busts and domestic abuse. The reports weren't just words and images to my senses. They were vivid reminders of a reality I could never forget. I knew that every one of the reports represented someone who was living through pain, heartache and a heavy sense of despair. I understood the feelings. I understood the people feeling them. That meant something.

It meant I had something I could offer to those who

75

were hurting like I once was. It also meant there was more to my life than shooting hoops. I had to do more, if only because I was someone who could.

I didn't know what the path looked like from where I stood in that beautiful home in the Canary Islands. But I knew the destination somehow involved me telling students who were suffering like I had that it was still possible to accomplish their dreams, no matter how hard life had been. I needed to tell them that they matter—and that their dreams matter—maybe more than they've ever been told.

I knew firsthand that life could seem hopeless, especially when you're living in a place nobody wants to live with the feeling that nobody cares what happens to you. Suddenly, I could no longer see my future in professional basketball. Instead, it was somewhere across the Atlantic, in front of the faces of kids who were ready to give up or maybe already had. They needed to know I believed in them—because I was once just like them.

In that moment I came to terms with being grateful that I'd bounced back from my horrific circumstances by becoming good at basketball. And then I came to terms with the fact that playing pro basketball was no longer my highest bounce. I knew I could do more than rise above my rough life; I could go back and help others rise above theirs too. That, I realized, would be the ultimate bounce. That would be a legacy I'd be proud of.

The next day, I called some of my family and friends and told them about my epiphany. Most of them thought I'd lost my mind. They reeled off the proof: I didn't have any connections in the speaking industry; I had never done anything besides play basketball; I had no experience, and it wasn't like I'd already made millions of dollars to live off of for the rest of my life.

"How are you gonna pay the bills, Chad?" they asked. "Why would you ever give up all that money to chase some crazy idea that just popped into your head? Who is going to hire you to speak anyway? Your story is nothing special. No one is going to care."

After listening to their tirades, I was left to ponder what it all meant. Were they right? As a husband and a father to two kids, was I being ridiculous or even irresponsible? Or was hearing this kind of response just the price of chasing a bigger dream?

I'd heard doubters all my life—that was nothing new. But that was when my dream didn't involve anyone else. This new dream, if it were real, would greatly affect three people I loved who were dependant on me to make the right decisions.

I treasured that night on the balcony as I finished out my second season in Spain. Teams from all over Europe had contacted my agent with contract offers worth more than double what I was already making. The contracts included additional performance incentives that would take the income even higher if I continued to excel.

Yet, as we packed up and headed home for our annual three-month break in my wife's hometown in Indiana, I wasn't thinking about the right team or the right contract or what I would do with all that money. As we flew across the Atlantic one more time, I wondered whether

I'd ever play basketball again.

I had been careful to make wise financial decisions. While in Europe, we were provided with everything needed—the house, the vehicles, and they even paid our taxes. We'd been careful not to overspend during our stateside break every year. It seemed as though I'd been preparing for this sudden transition all along.

But once we arrived in Indiana, the romance of my new dream began to wear off. I contemplated playing for another year or two, saving up a bunch of money and then going after this newfound purpose. It wasn't a bad idea—from a practical standpoint.

In the midst of my swirling thoughts, I headed to workout at a local gym. I spun the ball in front of me and started shooting jump shots. With every swish, I considered another sacrifice that giving up basketball would require. I thought of how we lived on the coast in Tenerife. I thought of the swimming pools, the tennis courts and the new SUV the team provided. I thought of the miniature golf course on the seventh floor of our resort where Cameron and Kiersten loved to play. I thought of the money that could allow my family to pursue their own dreams more easily.

I was twenty-five years old, injury-free and in the best shape of my life. I was embarking on the peak years of my basketball career. I was nowhere near retirement. I'd just signed with one of the top agents in the world. An endorsement deal with a major shoe company was in the works.

I reveled in the feeling of energy flowing through my

muscles as I dribbled up and down the court. I knew I was in the best shape of my life and playing at the best level I'd ever played—an NBA-playing level. I thought of playing before live crowds of tens of thousands of people and playing on television before millions.

I started shooting free throws, trying to make twenty-five in a row as I asked myself again and again if I could give up basketball. I thought back to high school and college, remembering all the sacrifices I had made to arrive where I was. I remembered cutting the cast off my broken hand, just two weeks into the six-week healing period, so I could force my hand into playing condition to be ready to play for my first team in Spain. Success had come with a price tag, and I had paid it in full and then some.

The risk would be huge if I were to start over and go after a new dream. I'd have to pay an even higher price than I'd already paid—a price that included giving up the game I loved, the game I'd leaned on my entire life.

I started running suicides up and down the court as I thought of a generation of young people who desperately needed a message of hope and encouragement—a generation that had, just a few months earlier, suffered through the tragic shooting at Columbine High School.

There was a war raging inside me.

I stopped running and dropped to my knees as sweat poured off my body. On that cool hardwood floor I searched for answers.

•••

Eventually, I accepted that I could not escape the pull of this new purpose inside me. It was not going away. Basketball had been my escape, my life, my dream. But basketball had served its purpose. It was a means to a greater end than merely lifting me beyond my rough childhood. It had taught me as much about success, discipline and pursuing my dreams than anything in my life. It had kept me from being swept up into the horrors of my upbringing and becoming a drug-user or abuser or simply a cynic with nothing good to say about life. I would be forever grateful for basketball. But now it was time to admit that rising up to become a pro basketball player had been a practice run for my biggest purpose of all.

At some point, everyone faces the decision between what is good and what is great. Basketball had been good to me. But it was only one step along the path to my greatest dream of all—to fulfill my purpose in life.

After that day in the gym, I stopped struggling with my decision. The sense of uncertainty was gone. While I knew the next step would be a challenge, I was confident it was the right step. I was choosing to pursue something great over simply accepting something good. It wasn't easy. But once I made the decision, an indescribable peace came over me.

I didn't have it all figured out, but the next day I called my agent and let him know I was officially done with basketball and that I was going to start an organization and speak to kids.

He said, "You're going to do what?"

"Speak to kids," I responded.

"Have you ever spoken before?"

"No, I've never spoken before."

"Do you have a degree in communications from the University of Pittsburgh?"

"No, it's actually in Social Sciences."

At that point I realized that he was mocking me, trying to make the point painfully clear that I didn't have any business doing what I was about to do. When he realized that I was not changing my mind, he cussed me out and hung up.

One of the contract offers that was on the top of my list was in Istanbul, playing for a Turkish team that was a perennial powerhouse. If I had accepted the contract, my family and I would have been living in the city when the 7.4 magnitude Izmit earthquake hit just outside the capital, killing an estimated 35,000 people and leaving a half-million homeless.

I don't know whether we'd have been killed, but I can tell you that the news padded my and Kristie's confidence that I'd made the right decision. At the very least, our lives would have been severely affected.

The real question on my mind was, "What now?" Basketball was my only source of income. While I had set aside plenty of finances to live comfortably for the three months we were home, my long-term plan hinged on signing a big contract for my third year. We would be able to do the things we'd talked about doing for years. Now, that security was gone and the money I had set aside for the summer dwindled as our stint in Indiana approached four-and-a-half months. The reality of our situation set in.

One day, feeling very agitated, I called Kristie and the kids into the living room of our apartment in Indiana. I told them to stand in a circle and hold hands. I didn't know what I was doing, but this felt right.

Kristie hadn't questioned me aloud once. Yet, I wondered if she was going to be able to have the faith to stand by me through all of this. She had grown up in a good home—not one where she had to worry about drugs or abuse or the next meal. I wondered if this situation was going to taint her trust in me. We were both becoming stressed because of the uncertainty of our future. I had no income and no job to speak of. What could I say to her right then? I searched for the words.

Then an odd idea hit me.

I turned to Kristie and said firmly, "Laugh."

She looked at me like I was a lunatic and said, "What?"

I shouted back, "Laugh!"

She reluctantly gave out a phony, "Ha. Ha. Ha."

I leaned in close and with the same fake tone said, "Ha. Ha. Ha."

Cameron and Kiersten didn't get it, but they must have thought Mom and Dad looked silly. They started to giggle.

Kristie and I looked at them, and then at each other. She cracked a smile—the kind of smile you get when you're sitting in class and you're not supposed to laugh. I saw it and she knew I saw it. We both burst out laughing. Soon, none of us could stop. It was as though the building uncertainty was now bursting out of us, not in anger or confusion or pain, but in genuine gut-felt amusement. I tumbled onto the floor and took Cameron down with me. Kiersten rolled on the floor squealing with delight. Soon Kristie joined us in a pile of laughter.

All the tension melted. All the agitation lifted. All the pressure disappeared.

I could have walked into that living room and said, "I have no idea what to do. Our rent is due in eight days and I don't have a plan." Or, Kristie could have challenged me to do something because our situation proved financially impossible. A heated argument could have arisen. Frustration, fear and pain could have ruled that moment. Instead, we chose to find joy in a time of adversity. It changed us.

It reminded us that no matter what, we could make it together. We had confidence, even if the path wasn't clear.

After our laughter finally subsided, I stood up and nodded to my family. It was time to bounce higher than I'd ever bounced before. I was going to leave the game I loved to chase a much bigger dream than I'd ever known before that day on the balcony. It was going to be scary and challenging. There were going to be a lot of doubters. But I was going to be okay—we were going to be okay—because I had already learned how to find the way.

•••

It has been more than a decade since I left basketball,

and I haven't regretted it for one second. Every day I am grateful that I didn't back down from that tough choice. If I had backed down, I wouldn't have been given the opportunity to stand before millions of teenagers facing circumstances just like mine—in some cases, even worse circumstances—and remind them that their dreams matter. If I had backed down, I wouldn't have been able to come to you completely confident that I can teach you what it really takes to reach your dreams.

There is a lot of hype out there today that claims it can make you rich, popular and famous. The vast majority of it is a waste of time and money. If you'll let me, I'd like to share with you what reaching your dreams really takes. The only warning I will give you is that by continuing to read this book, you are committing to a process of becoming the person you've always hoped you could be—the person you were made to be. Others might not recognize you when you're done. But you will. You've seen that person inside your heart all along.

KEYS TO REACHING YOUR DREAMS

8

DARE TO SHARE YOUR VISION

DARE TO SHARE YOUR VISION

When she was just nineteen months old, Helen Keller contracted a disease that many doctors believe was either scarlet fever or meningitis. It left her both blind and deaf. You've no doubt heard her story before today. Despite her limitations, and with the help of a selfless teacher named Anne Sullivan, she went on to become the first deaf/blind person to earn a Bachelor of Arts degree. From there she became a world-famous writer and speaker, and an active advocate for people with disabilities and for the working class. She was known for being someone who would not back down from pursuing something she believed in. In her younger years, she once asserted, "Life is either a daring adventure, or nothing." These are great words to live by. But something she said much later in her life might have been the most meaningful point she ever made when it comes to the topic of chasing after your dreams.

When asked if there was anything worse than living through life without the ability to hear or see, she immediately replied, "The only thing worse than being blind is having sight but no vision."

The vision she referred to was not the kind of vision that comes with a pair of working eyes. She was referring to the kind of vision that comes from a heart that has a dream for the future. Without that kind of vision, your life has no direction.

When I was very young and suffering through all my mom's dangerous choices, I didn't really have a vision for my future. I just wanted to survive another day. As I grew out of elementary school and into middle school, I began to understand that I had the power to change my circumstances. That compelled me to think about what I wanted my life to look like. By the time I was in eighth grade, I had locked in on a vision. When my homeroom teacher asked the class about our dreams, I shot my hand up and announced that I was going to play professional basketball. The other kids laughed aloud, but by then I was so certain about where I wanted my life to go that I sat up straighter in my chair and nodded. I had a picture of my future in mind, and I was committed to making it a reality one day.

The interesting thing that happened is that once I proclaimed my vision that day in eighth grade homeroom, something changed inside me. It was as though saying it out loud made it more real. Sure, I could have felt sorry for myself after that and decided to stop talking about it. I could have decided that those other kids laughing at me were right—my dream was a joke. But that isn't what happened, and it's not what will happen to you if the vision you dare to share is true to your heart.

If you truly believe in something, there is never any shame in sharing it with others. Of course, the older I got the more I learned that sharing my dreams with people I didn't trust or respect and expecting them to get it was foolish. They weren't following their dreams so there was no reason to expect them to believe or be excited about mine. But in the end, it didn't matter who believed in me and who didn't. I felt more and more empowered the more I shared this vision I had for my life. In a way, it was a form of accountability for my dreams. It was one thing to store up my thoughts inside my heart and head, but once I shared them with others, now they would be watching to see what would happen. Having those other sets of eyes observing me helped keep me motivated to do my best in school and practice and play basketball as often as I possibly could.

•••

The most important thing I want you to understand from the get-go is that your dreams can truly become a reality. As I said at the beginning of the book, every dreamer in the world—even the most famous ones— faced doubters once they decided to proclaim and pursue their dreams. The truth is that the world we live in was formed with those who saw a vision for their lives and set out to pursue it despite what others said, despite the odds. The Wright Brothers had a dream for aviation, and today we have jets that can fly us around the world. Thomas Edison had a dream to harness electricity, and today we have lights and power in our homes. Not all dreamers were inventors. Dr. Martin Luther King, Jr. was a different kind of dreamer who longed for a day when we would be judged by the content of our character and not the color of our skin. Today, because a man had a dream, we have an African American as President of the United States.

As long as there have been people on this planet, there have been dreams. And as long as there have been dreams, there have been doubters. Don't let the doubters stand in the way.

Consider the unfortunate plight of the president of Decca Records, a big doubter in the dream of four young British men who had formed a new band. In 1962, Decca had an opportunity sign the new group to the company's label, but when the man heard them he insisted he didn't like their sound and that guitars were "on their way out." That group was known as The Beatles.

Or consider a doubter who was once the president of the Digital Equipment Corporation. In 1977, he was given the opportunity to invest in the dream of a young man who wanted to create computers for people's homes. This company leader said, "There is no reason anyone would want a computer in their home." That young man he turned down is named Bill Gates, who kept chasing his dream and eventually created his own company called Microsoft.

Doubters are everywhere. Even the famous author of the Harry Potter series, J.K. Rowling, was initially told by an editor, "You'll never make any money out of children's books."

The real truth is that you'll never reach the destination you desire if you let the doubters keep you down. The moment you dare to share your dream with others is the moment doubters will appear and begin laughing and spouting their disapproval. Don't be surprised by them. The greatest dreamers of all time have faced the same challenges. Believe in your dream and power forward to make it a reality.

Tragically, our world is filled with people who only see the world for what it is and not what it can be. They never lift their eyes beyond their own circumstances to see what more they could become. That is not how achievers see things.

Achievers listen to their hearts and formulate a dream inside them for how their future can look. Then they look around and find the resources and opportunities that are needed to see that future happen.

Dare to dream. Then dare to share that dream with others. Not everyone will doubt you. The best around you will encourage you and help you reach your dream.

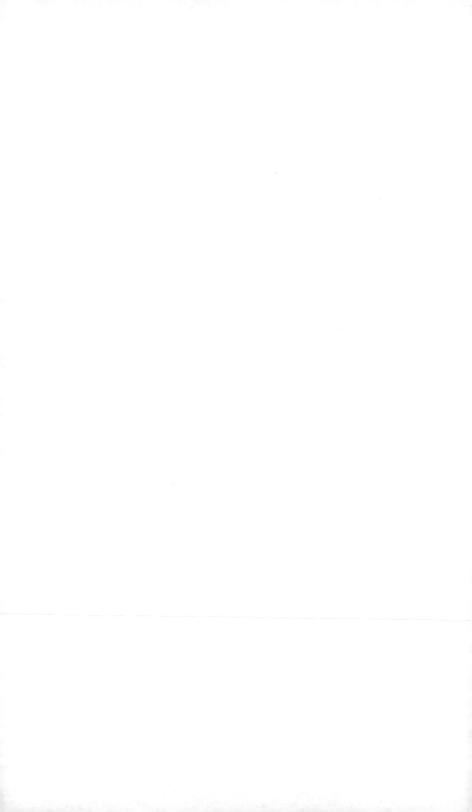

9

AVERAGE IS YOUR GREATEST ENEMY

AVERAGE IS YOUR GREATEST ENEMY

I remember lying in my bed when I was thirteen years old, staring at the ceiling, busted up and bruised by yet another of my mom's abusive boyfriends. I couldn't help but lose hope. I wanted to believe in a better future. I wanted to power forward, but I didn't know how much longer I could put up a good fight. I was at the end of my strength, and I felt like another incident could permanently tip the scales against my dreams.

What happened the next week was the last thing I expected.

I was walking home from an exhausting basketball practice. My muscles were sore from the second workout of the day. The sky was dark and dreary as I plodded along my neighborhood street. When I stepped into the door of our house, I immediately noticed it was dark and quiet. I tossed my bag over the kitchen chair.

"Mom? You home?"

There was no answer.

I looked in the fridge for some food. Nothing looked good. I wandered into the living room to watch TV. That's when I saw her.

My mom was passed out and sprawled across our beat-up gray couch. Her clothes were a mess, and as I got closer to her, I could see the alcohol and drug paraphernalia on the coffee table and floor.

My heart jumped into my throat. You have to understand that when I was thirteen, I was already sick of the alcohol and drug scene. I didn't need a teacher or a motivational speaker to give me statistics on the dangers of substance abuse. I didn't need anyone to try and convince me to stay away from the party lifestyle. I'd seen the effects firsthand. I was fed up.

I nudged my mom awake with my foot and pointed at the mess.

"What are you doing, Mom? Are you using again?"

The moment she heard those words, a switch flipped inside her. Her eyes turned dark and she started yelling at me, accusing me of pouring her alcohol down the sink and flushing her drugs down the toilet. It was something Wendy and I had done in the past, trying to protect her. She jumped up from the couch and swung at me with her fist clinched, just missing my face and hitting me in the right shoulder. I knew she was really messed up because to that point in my life, it was rare for her to be physically violent toward me.

After she missed me, she turned and ran into the kitchen, screaming an old familiar tirade.

"You don't love me! You never have!"

Her tone caused a chill to run up my spine.

As she rushed back toward me, I looked down at her hand. It was squeezing the handle of a large butcher knife. It was meant for me.

I sped to the other side of the living room, then back into the kitchen through the other hallway. She ran after me, swinging the knife as we raced in and out of the kitchen several times. It was a small house and she was never more than a few feet behind me. I managed to avoid her for several passes—until I tried to open the heavy wood front door without letting up speed.

As I reached to pull down on the door's lever, my mom lunged at me and swung the knife at my arm. It sliced deeply into my wrist until the blade hit bone. I fell on the kitchen floor and watched in slow motion as my own blood sprayed on the stove, cabinets and linoleum floor.

Instinctively, I jumped up and she chased me through the house once again. Fortunately the front door had swung open and I busted through the screen door, breaking it off its hinges. I threw it aside and began sprinting down my street, Marion Crescent Boulevard. My mom chased me down the block with the knife swinging at her side. I took a right on West Chicago Boulevard and ran with everything I had. In the open I was able to outrun her, and she finally disappeared.

When I saw that she had turned back, I stopped running. Panting, I pressed on the gushing wound with my other hand. Blood was still pouring out as I bent over and tried to determine what to do.

I walked to Telegraph Road and found a pay phone at the Mobil gas station. I dialed my cousin Tim's number and was relieved when he answered.

"Tim, you gotta come get me."

He hurried to pick me up and took me to the hospital where we told the nurses and doctors that we were messing around and I accidently got cut. I don't know if they believed our story, but nobody asked questions. They just stitched me up. Afterward we discussed where I should go. I insisted my mom would be passed out at that point and that I would be fine going back home.

"What if she comes to?" Tim asked.

"She's gonna be out for hours," I said. "Trust me, I know the routine."

"I'd feel better if you came home with me," he replied.

"You know that won't work. There isn't room. Your parents have company staying this week. Plus there'd be a lot of embarrassing questions. Please, man, I don't want the hassle."

"Okay," he agreed. "But I'm coming with you."

We arrived back at my house and approached the side door, which opened up to the stairs that led to the basement and my bedroom. I opened the door slowly, and we eased into the house. Before heading downstairs, we peaked around the wall into the living room. Sure enough, there was my mom, completely blacked out and lying by the fireplace.

We headed down the stairs and I told Tim he could

sleep on the couch. I found him a sleeping bag and then settled under my covers and flipped out the lamp on my nightstand. We talked for about an hour and then Tim fell asleep. Like most nights, I couldn't sleep. I just lay there in my bed, thinking about how miserable my life was. I picked up my arm, which looked like a club with all the bandaging they had put on it at the hospital. *What am I going to tell my teachers and friends tomorrow at school?* I thought to myself. *What story am I going to make up this time?*

It was at this moment that I started thinking about what my mom's boyfriends had always told me. They used to look me dead in my eyes and tell me I was "worthless" and that I "would never amount to anything." They told me I had the same personality traits as them and would end up just like them. They used to mock me and tell me that it was a fairytale if I thought I would ever make it out of Detroit through basketball.

I stared into the dark, replaying those words over and over again. A fire rose inside of me. I didn't want to be like everybody told me I was going to be. I wanted to be successful and make something of my life.

I squeezed the hand of my bandaged arm into a fist and shook it.

I know there's a purpose for my life, my heart cried out.

I'm not giving up! I mouthed to the darkness.

Hot tears ran down my cheeks. I believed it. I believed my life mattered and had a purpose—even if I couldn't see it clearly.

In an unexpected twist, that horrible encounter was a tipping point—but not away from my dreams. It pushed me closer to the commitment I needed to make.

I had finally come face to face with my mom's demons—the same demons that had tried to take me out my entire life.

I knew the woman who carved that butcher knife into my arm wasn't my mom—not the mom that I knew she was deep down. It was the personification of the forces that had been trying to kill my dreams since I was born. I had now looked into their eyes. I'd felt them cut deeply into my flesh. I wasn't about to back down.

In the days that followed, I continued trying to persuade my mom to get help once again, convinced that somehow she would get clean. But our relationship began to change as I made the decision once and for all that I wasn't going to become a statistic. I wasn't going to be like all the other kids who grew up like I did and ended up just like their parents, or worse. I was going to rise higher than the expectations surrounding me.

That was the night I realized my greatest enemy wasn't my circumstances or my mom's choices or even my age. My greatest enemy was average. I began to understand that if I was going to realize my dreams I had to be and do more than the average kid in my circumstances.

The same is true for you.

Everyone who has ever lived can find a reason to settle for average. Life is very hard at times. We get burned out, tired, exhausted, afraid, frustrated, defeated, lost, scared and hopeless. We all have these feelings at some point. They make us want to give up, stop fighting, settle for something less than the best.

I've been there. I've been kicked, beaten and bruised by what this life dishes out. I have scars and wounds that may fade with time, but they'll never completely go away.

So do you.

Despite all the doubters and difficult circumstances you might face, average is your greatest enemy because it's the only enemy you can personally defeat. You can't always control the forces around you—things like who your parents are and what choices they make or where you live and whether or not you have any money. But you can control your response to the forces around you. It's not always easy, but how you react remains your choice. You can let the forces shape you, or you can refuse to let something or someone else control who you become.

Your surroundings often act like a funnel, trying to squeeze you into a clone of the others around you. The pull of peer pressure is to fit in, dress the same, act the same and even misbehave the same. But the promise of peer pressure—that you will be successful if you fit in—is a lie. It's a lie because the people who go on to achieve great things are never clones of those around them. They are unique, one-of-a-kind individuals. That's because every dream inside a person is unique, and if your dream is unique, you must be too in order to see it happen.

You have to be willing to do things others won't do. You have to think things others don't think. You have to be willing to say no when they say yes. This doesn't mean you have to be an outcast to be great at something. It just means that you can't get your cues on how to look or talk or think from those around you. Those cues should come from the dreams inside your heart.

The message here is straightforward: If you want to achieve something great in life, you have to strive to be more than an ordinary, average person. The old saying is true: If you keep doing what you've always done, you will keep getting what you've always gotten. Instead, be unique. Be uncommon. Rise above average and become an extraordinary person.

10

SUCCESS IS A CHOICE

SUCCESS IS A CHOICE

Do you remember when I had that huge game in high school and all my teammates wanted me to come party with them? I told them I couldn't because I still had some work to do. Then I got in the car with my dad and drove home. I didn't tell you the rest of the story that night.

As my dad started the engine, he looked at me and said, "Chad, you just had an incredible game. You should be soaring with enthusiasm. What's wrong?"

"Nothing," I said. "The guys are just giving me a hard time because I won't go out and party with them."

"So what did you tell them?"

"I just told them I had some work to do."

My dad looked at me funny but said nothing more. He knew I wasn't a partier, but I'm sure he was wondering what kind of work I intended to do at 11:30 p.m. in the seedy section of Detroit where my mom and I lived.

The truth is that I had just scored 57 points and had 18 rebounds—but I wasn't finished working on my dream. Once home, I changed into a new pair of shorts and threw on a long sleeve t-shirt and hoodie. After tying my running shoes, I walked out the front door into the cool night air. I started stretching under a dim streetlight, thinking over the game. I then took off on a three-mile run—not a wise thing to do in an area known for being the nation's murder capital. But it's what I had to do.

As my feet hit the pavement with each stride, I thought about how I wanted to accomplish so much more than scoring 57 points in a high school basketball game. I wanted to be the first in my family to get a college degree. I wanted to play pro basketball. And I wanted to have a family of my own and create a completely different life for them than the one I had known.

• • •

As young kids, we are extremely resilient. Despite the forces against us, despite the evidence pointing to a hopeless future, we are somehow able to keep believing in our dreams. Then at some point, often in middle or high school, it becomes more difficult to shun the constant message of our circumstances—that we are bound to be nothing more than a product of our environment. After hearing that gloomy message for years, it becomes difficult to believe in the hopeful message of our dreams. It can even seem foolish to keep your hope alive. And yet, when those feelings begin to arise, that's when you can know the road you choose really matters.

Many times in your life, you will be faced with the choice to either keep pursuing your dreams or lose hope and let life happen to you. I can tell you that despite the worst circumstances imaginable or the biggest mistakes you've ever made, there is always a reason to keep fighting. Your dreams are at the center of that reason. They are not childish fantasies. And they are no accident.

You are here on this earth for a specific reason—it is the key to your life making sense and your days bringing you joy and satisfaction. The fact is that only you can do what you are made to do in the unique way you are made to do it. The dreams inside you are the compass pointing your life down its best path. Don't ignore that compass. Don't pass your dreams off as impossible or impractical. Choose them, every day, regardless of your age.

Frank Sinatra began singing for tips when he was only eight years old.

Tiger Woods began swinging a golf club when he was three years old.

Beethoven played his first public concert at seven years old.

Serena Williams started playing tennis at five years old.

It's never too early to begin.

Choose to follow your dreams today, no matter how high the mountain or how deep the valley is before you. Don't assume the path should be easy. While the rewards of fulfilling your dreams will be worth far more than the price you pay along the way, choosing success is never easy. There will be challenges. Forces will rise up to block your way and try to divert you down another path. These forces will insist that you can't accomplish all you have in your heart to accomplish. Overcoming them is no cakewalk. It is also not impossible. You can rise up and defeat them no matter who or what they are. You must, if you will achieve your dreams.

Despite what magazines and movies might tell you, success is not easy and it's not a matter of luck. There are no shortcuts or quick fixes to greatness. The day after winning his first NBA Championship, Michael Jordan went to a gym and started working on his jump shot. He'd been told that he couldn't shoot very well—he could only drive to the basket and dunk. While all his teammates were on vacation celebrating their success, Jordan was back at work. He wanted more than one championship. He wanted to be known for being more than just a freak athlete that could dunk. He wanted to be the best player to ever play the game. That, he knew, took a daily choice. Over the course of his career, Jordan became not only known for his great shooting from any range; he also became the best defensive player in the game and led his teams to six NBA Championships.

No matter what your dreams entail, being successful at them is a daily choice to do whatever is necessary. You have to win each day, one day at a time. When you string enough daily victories together, your life begins to look like you've dreamed it could. You also become far less willing to surrender. Eventually, your daily victories culminate in your dreams becoming your reality.

Simply put: Success is a choice. You must deserve your dreams. You have to earn them. That means you must choose to chase them every day.

11

LEARN TO FAIL FORWARD

LEARN TO FAIL FORWARD

There is no such thing as success without failure. No matter who you are, the road to success is littered with mistakes. Even the most successful people in history had multiple failures before they finally succeeded.

Colonel Sanders, the founder of KFC, thought restaurant owners would love his fried chicken recipe and want to use it. He drove around the country wearing his white suit, knocking on doors, sleeping in his car. Do you know how many times people said no before he got one yes? One thousand and nine times.

While the famous slugger Babe Ruth hit 714 home runs in his career, he struck out nearly twice as many times during the same span—1,330 times to be exact.

Abraham Lincoln was a perpetual failure. When he was twenty-two, he failed in business. When he was twenty-three, he ran for the State Legislature and lost. When he was twenty-four, he failed in business again.

The following year he was elected to the Legislature. When he was twenty-six, his sweetheart died. At the age of twenty-seven, he had a nervous breakdown. When he was twenty-nine, he was defeated for the post of Speaker of the House in the State Legislature. When he was thirty-one, he was defeated as Elector. When he was thirty-four, he ran for Congress and lost. At the age of thirty-seven, he ran for Congress and finally won. Two years later, he ran again and lost his seat in Congress. At the age of forty-six, he ran for the U.S. Senate and lost. The following year he ran for Vice President and lost that, too. He ran for the Senate again, and lost again. Finally, at the age of fifty-one, he was elected President of the United States.

Walt Disney—the man who gave us Disney World and Mickey Mouse—was fired by a news editor because he "lacked imagination." He then went bankrupt trying to build his first animation company. Legend has it he was turned down 302 times before he finally got the financing to create Disney World.

Before he won the Nobel Prize and his name became synonymous with the word genius, Albert Einstein's parents, teachers and peers believed he had a mental handicap because he didn't speak until he was four years old. Later, he was expelled from high school for being rebellious.

• • •

Hearing the truth about failure was important for a kid like me who had seen very little success in life. It meant that if I learned from my mistakes and kept trying, I could still taste success. My dad tried to instill this in me from a young age, but that doesn't mean it sunk in right away. In fact, it wasn't until I had graduated from the University of Pittsburgh that I fully comprehended the value of failing forward.

If you recall, I told you that an injury to my hand forced me to change my plans to play in the NBA and instead play in Europe. What I didn't tell you is how I sustained that injury. It was one of the biggest failures of my life.

Kristie and I, along with young Cameron, had moved back to Michigan where I was preparing for the Mavericks training camp every day at a local gym. What happened two days before the start of the NBA summer leagues changed everything.

That morning I headed to the gym in Taylor, Michigan to work out with a friend. Sometime in the middle of our workout, my mom came in.

I took a break and walked over to greet her.

"Chad, I'm finally doing it," she blurted out. "I'm not going to be abused anymore. I'm pressing charges and I need you to come with me to the courthouse for support. Will you do that?"

I hesitated for a moment because it was something I hadn't thought about in a while. Life with my mom seemed far behind me—especially now that I was married and had a son of my own. Still, I wanted to support her.

I left my stuff with my friend and told him I'd be back in an hour.

My mom and I arrived at the courthouse and walked inside. Before we entered the courtroom, the clerk stopped us and told me I couldn't go in.

"What?" I said. "Why?"

"You have to be dressed appropriately for the court," the man explained, looking at my tank top and shorts.

I looked down at my sweaty clothes and agreed.

"Mom, I'll be right outside. Don't worry, you'll do fine."

When they brought her boyfriend in, I watched through the small window in the door, hoping she'd have the strength to share the full details. My heart quickly sank as I observed my mom letting fear get the best of her. I could see that she was telling very little of what he'd done. Her boyfriend got off with only a restraining order.

I groaned as she walked out of the courtroom door. Her boyfriend was close behind. He swaggered past me to a counter where they had to sign some documents. While the three of us stood there waiting for the paperwork, the boyfriend walked over to me and leaned in.

"Whaddaya gonna do now, big boy?" he said quietly.

"Yeah, you're a real man," I shot back. "You can beat up a woman."

"You bet I can," he taunted, "and that's just what I'm going to do as soon as I get her back to the house. I'm gonna teach her a lesson for all this trouble she caused me."

Suddenly all the sights and sounds of my mom's abuse overloaded the circuits in my brain. Every muscle in my body tightened.

The boyfriend smirked at me. With every ounce of power in me, I catapulted my right fist at his face. At the last second he turned his head. Instead of hitting his jaw, my knuckles slammed into the back of his head. I could feel the bones inside my hand snap.

Security was all over us within seconds. They began to handcuff me. Then the lady behind the counter spoke up.

"Don't be taking him away!" she yelled. "You want to lock somebody up, take him." She pointed to the boyfriend.

The officers believed her, and they let me go. Unfortunately, the anger inside me had not run its course.

I jumped into my car and raced back to the gym to get my friend. Then we headed back toward the courthouse. I pulled the car up to a curb a few blocks away. I knew the boyfriend would be walking to my mom's house as soon as they let him leave.

Within minutes, I saw him coming. The minute he was within reach I jumped out of the car and began fighting with him. I thought of all the times I'd seen my mom busted up and bleeding. I wanted him to feel every bit of pain she had ever felt. I wanted him to feel the fear and anguish Wendy and I had felt night after night because of guys like him. I whaled on him over and over until the rage in me subsided. He was bloodied and dazed and laid out on the sidewalk when I finally stood up, hopped back in the car and drove off.

A mile down the road the reality of what I'd done

sunk in. I dropped off my friend and raced home to Kristie.

"We've got to go," I insisted the moment I stepped inside. "Come on."

"Chad, what are you doing?" she said.

"Come on! I'm in big trouble. We've got to go. Right now!"

Confused and frightened, Kristie scooped up one-year-old Cameron and jumped into the car.

"What happened? Where are we going?" she pleaded as we sped down the highway.

"Listen, don't ask me any questions right now; I'm too shook up. We're going to a friend's house. I'll tell you everything when we get there."

I could tell that Kristie was really worried. Ten miles later, I took a deep breath and told her everything.

That night, with my broken hand in a cast, I remember confessing to Kristie over and over, "I don't ever want to react like that again." I had let the violence I despised for so many years take root inside me. Now the pain it caused and the damage it did to me was unmistakable. I knew what I had to do.

I made two phone calls the next morning. The first was to find out what charges had been filed against me.

"You won't believe this," my mom said. "He couldn't press charges!"

"What? You're crazy," I told her.

"No, really, Chad. He ran straight back to the court-house, bleeding and crying, and they told him as far as they were concerned he deserved it and to get out. No charges were filed."

The second phone call was to my agent.

"You did what?" he barked. Once he calmed down, he sighed and then conceded, "Well, we'll just have to look at some other options."

• • •

Through that experience I finally understood that life is a process, not an event. And a process is always marked by successes and failures. That's important to know because it's easy to get down whenever you experience a setback from your dreams—especially when that setback is something you thought you'd conquered. It's one thing when you get caught in circumstances you couldn't control. It's another thing when you bring the circumstances on yourself. Then it's hard not to beat yourself down. If it happens enough, it's tempting to believe that nothing will ever change because you cannot get beyond your own shortcomings.

However, being resilient and bouncing back higher demands that you take ownership of who you are and what you do—the good and the bad—and keep moving forward. That means that while you must always strive to improve, you should also give yourself room to fail. I'm not talking about making excuses. I'm talking about pushing yourself as hard as you possibly can while maintaining the perspective that you will still make mistakes, sometimes big ones.

What you do when you fail is one of the most critical factors in your future success. The first thing you should do is not panic. There's no reason for you to panic when you know that every successful person has failed numerous times. The second thing you should do is step back, survey the scene and take ownership of what you did and what the actions revealed about you. Then you should take immediate action in a better direction. That's how you fail forward. You don't wait to feel better about yourself. You don't wait for the dust to settle or the situation to somehow fix itself. You do what you have to do right away.

Remember that the key to success is not in never failing; it is in rising higher each time you hit the floor. In fact, you couldn't learn to bounce if you weren't thrown down once in a while. As long as there is breath in your lungs, you need to hold on to the truth that failure is not fatal. In the end, the greatness of your life is in direct proportion to your willingness to keep fighting for what you believe in despite the missteps along the way. Do that consistently, for long enough, and your success will far outweigh your failures.

12

HARD WORK ALWAYS PAYS OFF

HARD WORK ALWAYS PAYS OFF

Before I left to play my first year in the Big East—the number one conference in the nation at the time—I told everybody back home and at Vincennes that I was going to be a starter my first year. I knew I had the skills; after all, I was an All-American.

Arriving on campus, I realized that unlike high school ball or playing at the junior college level where I stood out, at Pittsburgh just about everyone on the team was a former high school or junior college All-American. Unlike high school ball, where only a few players were willing to go the extra mile in training, I found myself playing with a team full of talented players who were determined to be the best. It took a lot to be willing to do what the other guys wouldn't because training at the major college level was already grueling. It was like they had a license to kill us, and we didn't even get paid. Hard work, persistence and tunnel vision became instilled in me.

We were in the middle of two-a-day practices—mornings and evenings—when I found myself competing for a starting position against a veteran team member. We were a running, up and down, full-court pressing team and it didn't take me long to see that the player I was up against had some serious advantages over me. He was older, had more experience playing in the Big East than me and was physically more developed.

Running sprints and suicides one morning in Fitzgerald Field House, my muscles burning, I wondered if it had been such a wise idea to brag to everyone at home that I'd have a starting position.

Finally, coach changed his monologue from a relentless, "Don't quit! Run! Suck it up!" to, "Alright, hit the showers." I was looking forward to the hot tub, the training table of food and a chance to rest before the evening practice. I walked down the stairs toward the locker room, and the teammate I was competing against for that starting position was right in front of me. I stopped dead in my tracks. My words to everyone back home echoed in my head. I knew they would never come true unless I was willing to work harder than the player in front of me. I turned around and headed back up to the court.

"Hey!" I called out to one of the team managers. "Would you mind staying an extra twenty or thirty minutes to rebound for me?"

"Sure," he agreed.

My habits changed from that day on. I stayed after practice day after day, working on my jump shot, my ball handling and my free throws. I came to a point where I wouldn't leave the court until I made at least ten free throws in a row. My legs burned just as bad as the other guys' after practice, but I knew if I wanted to be successful and reach my dream, I had to be willing to do things the other guy wasn't doing. I had to work harder than him.

When it came time for our coach to announce the starters, I won the starting position. And I never lost it. It was no fluke or mistake. I deserved it. I simply worked harder than the other guy. I shot more jump shots than he did. I dribbled more. I ran more. I sweated more. I bled more. I pushed myself in ways that he didn't. What I learned in the process is that hard work always pays off.

•••

When you follow the Twitter feeds of today's most successful people, it's tempting to believe that success is easy and the process of getting there is glamorous. These people are spending money here and jet-setting there. Collaborating with other stars. Attending fancy events and driving expensive cars. It seems like a perfect life of maximum pleasure with minimum effort. What you rarely read or hear about is the hard work going on behind all those popular Twitter feeds: the twenty-hour workdays...the two hundred days a year on the road...the constant meetings...the frequent nights in hotels...and the daily grind of rehearsing or practicing or running a company a little bit better than the rest of the competition. The truth is that just about anyone could make his life seem easy and glamorous if all you saw were the rewards of hard work.

When I made the decision to pursue a career as a professional speaker, I knew that I was making the decision to live a lot of my life on the road, including being a husband and father. Because of my childhood, I was determined not to repeat my past, and Kristie and I made the decision that I was not going to travel alone. They were coming with me. We raised Cameron and Kiersten on the road, homeschooling them through middle school so we could be together as a family. It was anything but easy. But we knew that success in anything requires hard work. Making our family the number one priority would be no different. I certainly could have made my life seem glamorous if all I did was tweet pictures of the huge crowds I was speaking to and the celebrities I was meeting and the glamorous parts of the different cities I was staying in every month. But that wouldn't tell the real story. That would be a fantasy.

It's the great lie of today's modern culture that you can have the rewards of success without paying the proper price. Success is not a door you walk through; it's a spiral staircase that you have to climb day after day. Success isn't cheap. It isn't easy. But it's worth it when you truly put in the time. Wanting a great family, a big house, a luxury car or a million dollars in the bank is all very nice, but the problem is that practically everyone wants these things. When it comes to success, the big question isn't: "What do you want?" The big question is: "How hard are you willing to work to get what you want?" Most people only consider the first question.

On the other hand, successful people find out what it's going to cost to make their dreams come true. Then they find a way to make it happen. Most importantly, they don't complain about all the hard work. They accept it as the price they must pay.

The truth is that you will always place a higher value on the things for which you have worked hard—like your first car or an "A" in a tough class or a spot on the varsity team. These achievements matter more than the things that just come easy. The side of success that is promoted far less today is the blood, sweat and tears that go into achieving a dream. Many people like to promote the rewards of success without acknowledging the work that it requires.

No matter what you read or hear, there are no short-cuts to realizing your dreams. I understand how the message of simple success has become so believable today, but it's the furthest thing from the truth. And the unfortunate reality is that those who buy into that message are ultimately buying into something much more dangerous. It's called apathy.

These days, most people don't want to work hard. Apathy rules the majority. It's all about how little you can do and still manage to get by. It's all about trying to succeed with as little effort as possible. It's about looking like success comes easy for you. Sadly, most people believe it's more important to look good than to give the maximum effort. They think it's more important to keep their clothes clean and their foreheads dry.

I can tell you that in all my years of living I have never met a person who held those beliefs and ended up being successful. Most of them end up living with remorse. Many end up depressed. Some end up in prison doing time for their so-called shortcuts to success.

The irony is that whether you decide to work hard for what you want or try to find a shortcut, you will end up putting in your time. If you decide to take the lazy route, you might get some more sleep today, but you will eventually put in your time with many future days of disappointment and regret. If you decide to work hard today, you'll put in your time now with blood, sweat and tears, and soon you'll be reaping your reward while everyone else is wondering why they gave up so soon.

Years ago, an author named Napoleon Hill wrote about a man who traveled to California during the 1849 Gold Rush.[1] Like many of the prospectors there, he was hoping to immediately strike it rich and never have to work again. For months the man rose early and spent all day chipping away at the surrounding hills with his pickaxe and shovel. While he found small flakes of gold here and there, it was nothing that would make him rich. He kept digging, convinced his fortune was out there.

Then one day, he couldn't dig any more. He lost heart, put down his tools and gave up.

Upon hearing the man had given up, another prospector working nearby offered to buy his tools. The first man agreed and made back what money he could.

The new prospector then hired three men to study

the land and determine where the big deposit of gold was most likely to be. They pointed the prospector to a spot that was three feet from where the previous man had quit digging. When the new prospector dug there, he soon struck an enormous deposit of gold.

The story is a good reminder of what often happens when you refuse to keep working hard and give up on your dreams too soon. Like the first prospector, you might be a few feet from reaching your dreams and not realize it. And the only way you will ever know is if you keep digging in.

The interesting thing about dreams is that when you finally reach them and look back on the road you took to get there, you realize that your journey to success was in some ways just as enjoyable as the reward of arriving at your desired destination. Most people call this the "thrill of the chase," and it's the reason so many successful people reach one dream and immediately begin chasing after another—much like I did. The truth is that the harder you work for what you want, the sooner you realize you can accomplish much more than you originally thought.

When you're facing tough times...keep on chasing your dream.

When people point their fingers...keep pressing forward.

When the pressure is on...keep climbing higher.

When everything on the inside and outside is screaming at you to quit...dig deep, grit your teeth and refuse to let anything keep you from reaching your dream.

Before you know it, you will.
And then you'll begin chasing the next dream.

[1]Napoleon Hill, *Think and Grow Rich*. Fawcett Crest, 1960.

13

GET OVER THE FEAR OF WHAT OTHER PEOPLE THINK

GET OVER THE FEAR OF WHAT OTHER
PEOPLE THINK

My mom had a habit of leaving the house in perfect order before she left. I'll never forget the time our entire family—my mom, dad, Wendy and I—had moved back to Detroit from Cincinnati. I was eleven, and it was after the best season our family had ever known. We had no reason to think our life together wouldn't continue to improve. Then my dad, Wendy and I walked into our house one afternoon and came upon a living room and kitchen so clean you could eat off the floor. We knew our mom had left us again and there was no way of knowing where she'd gone or when she'd return.

She'd been working to help pay our bills, and so with her gone we were forced to move in with my dad's mom, Grandma Varga. There was little room for all three of us so Wendy eventually moved in with our Grandma Little, our mom's mom. I hated being separated from Wendy.

My dad and I shared a room at Grandma Varga's

house and it was in this setting, several months after my mom left without warning, that I was startled awake at three in the morning.

I rubbed my eyes and I glanced over to my dad's bed. He wasn't there. Instead, he was on the floor, next to the bed, sobbing uncontrollably.

"Dad, what is it?" I said as I leapt out of my bed.

"I don't know, Son," he choked. "It's your mom. I just feel like something is happening with your mom."

I wrapped an arm around him and together we talked for what seemed like an hour. Finally, my dad said, "Chad, you know your mom left that muffled message on Grandma Little's answering machine last week saying something about being in Atlanta, right?"

"Yeah, but that was like a week ago," I replied. "Who knows where she could be now?"

"I know, Son. I know," he said softly and then paused a moment. "I know this sounds absolutely crazy, but I just have this sense that we need to go to Atlanta and find your mom."

It was as though saying it out loud had confirmed something in him. He took me firmly by the shoulders and said, "Somehow, Son, we have to go get your mom."

We went back to bed that night wondering what the next day would bring. We didn't have any money. We didn't even have a car to get there, and this wasn't a city down the road. It was Georgia. We were in Michigan, over seven hundred miles away.

The following morning I woke to someone shaking me.

"Son!"

I shot up.

"We overslept," my dad asserted. "Get ready quick—church starts in half an hour."

I threw on my Sunday clothes, pushed my feet into my worn out penny loafers and raced to the kitchen to grab a piece of toast as my dad and I headed out the door.

"How are we gonna do it, Dad?" I asked breathlessly as we quickly made our way to my grandma's car.

"I don't quite know yet, Chad. I need to talk it over with some of my friends."

After the service, I watched my dad head down the main aisle toward one of his friends. Just then another man crossed my dad's path and stopped him. He handed my dad an envelope and shook his hand. Inside the envelope was two hundred dollars. The man confessed he didn't know why he was doing it but felt a strong sense that he should.

My dad stared at the envelope in wonder. Then he looked up and walked confidently toward his friend. I headed to the foyer to await our fate.

Soon an arm dropped across my shoulder. My dad looked down at me, "Well, Son, it means doing free lawn work all summer for your grandmother's best friend, Frances, but we have the use of her car for the next three days."

"So we're going?" I asked.

"Of course we're going." He grinned at me as we walked out of the church.

The cold stares slapped us in the face the moment we stepped outside. Somehow, word of my dad's plan to go to Atlanta had already spread. Friends and family were gathered and ready to lay into us.

"What are you doing, Don?" one aunt screeched.

"Are you out of your mind?" a friend spouted. "After all the times Kathie has cheated and lied, what reason on earth could you have for wanting to bring her back?"

More sneers of disappointment and jabs of disbelief ensued. I looked over at my dad. He was just standing there, shoulders forward and eyes down.

"This is just another financial blunder, Don," an older relative said, pointing at the holes in my penny loafers. "Just look at Chad's shoes. Now that's what you should be using that money for."

I could feel the blood rising to my face.

"Yes," someone else agreed. "And what about Wendy, Don? Did you stop to think of her? She needs clothes, Don, not her father going off on some wild goose chase!"

Finally I'd had enough. With my fists clenched I stood tall.

"Stop it!" I shouted. "All of you! Just stop it!"

Several others had crowded around by this time. It seemed like there were a hundred people standing there against us. I didn't care.

"We have to go," I asserted. "You don't understand. You didn't see my dad last night."

I looked around for a sign that anyone understood. They just shook their heads as my dad led me away to the borrowed car.

His pain was visible on his face as we pulled the car doors shut. I watched him slowly slide the seat belt across his lap and lock it in place. He then leaned back against the seat and passed his hand through his hair. He glanced down at my shoes and shook his head.

He then closed his eyes. He kept them closed for about ten seconds.

When he opened his eyes it was clear a change had taken place. The blood that had drained from his face began to return. He squared his shoulders and sat up straight. He took in a deep breath and blew it out. Placing his right hand on my shoulder, he gave it a firm squeeze and then looked me in the eye.

"Son, we're going to Atlanta."

The Pontiac 6000 roared to life and we sped out of the parking lot, heading due south. We eventually settled into long silence as our car passed over the next state line and the next. Inside, both of us were wondering the same thing, *How can we possibly find anyone in a city the size of Atlanta*?

We crashed in a motel not far from the city. The following morning we rose early and finished the drive. The closer we got, the more disillusioned I became. My dad could see it in my posture.

"Come on, Chad. We can do this," he said as we approached an exit just outside of Atlanta. We took the off-ramp and turned right. I started looking for a Wendy's so I could get the Frosty my dad had promised. Suddenly, he flipped off the radio. Silence filled the car. I looked at his face. He was staring intently at something across the road. I followed his gaze and leaned forward to see better. A lady wearing a light blue shirt and cutoff jean shorts was running down the opposite side of the road. Her bleached-blond hair was flying behind her. My mouth fell open. I shot a look at my dad as we yelled in unison.

"Mom!"

My dad sped forward and flipped a u-turn at the first available chance. We were yelling with delight. My dad sped up behind her and then yanked the car off the road and slammed on the brakes. I jumped out of the car and took off running.

"Mom!" I screamed. "Mom! It's Chad, stop!"

She didn't turn around.

She ran even faster.

A thousand thoughts assaulted my mind, all with the same message. *How could we have been so stupid to think she cared about us?*

Somehow I kept running, faster and faster, tears blurring my vision.

"Mom!" I cried out again. "Please stop!"

Finally, she glanced over her shoulder and caught sight of me.

She immediately stopped running and turned around.

I could see her eyes widen. She began running toward me with her arms open wide. She was crying when we reached each other. We collapsed in a heap on the side of the road, and my dad soon joined us. He was crying too.

• • •

In the ensuing days, we learned what had happened to her.

She had hitchhiked out of Michigan when she left us. One car after another, she headed for Florida, using drugs along the way, until a guy from Georgia picked her up and convinced her to join him. He was running a crack house in Atlanta. Soon she was trapped in an abusive relationship with him.

Then one night the guy's sister told my mom that he had grown tired of the relationship. She knew too much and he was going to kill her. The sister advised my mom to leave immediately.

Early the next morning, my mom snuck out of the house and took off running. She didn't stop until a few miles later when she heard her son calling her name near an expressway off-ramp.

• • •

My mom returned to Michigan with us but this time she didn't move in. She entered rehab instead—it was a turning point in her journey, thanks to my dad's faith and willingness to take a stand for something that was on his heart to do. As my mom fought hard to beat down the enemies of her dreams, I stood taller knowing that any dream was possible for those who didn't fear what others thought.

• • •

Whenever you stand up for something you believe in, the critics will stand up next. The world is full of people who spend their lives picking apart the dreams of others so they don't have to face their own shortcomings and disappointments. Most of them don't even know that's why they are doing it, but sadly, when people aren't chasing their dreams, they don't want to hear about you chasing yours. Your hard work and persistence become a tangible source of pain in their lives. You become a constant reminder of what they should have done and could have done but didn't. So they spout off about how silly or naïve or stupid you are to take away their own pain.

If you listen to their voices and let them fill your heart with fear, embarrassment or shame, you'll end up just like them. Bitter, cynical and full of regret. Don't fall prey to the petty words of cynics. Don't fear what their words will do because they are ultimately powerless to change your course unless you let them. Fear paralyzes your dreams—never let fear win.

Through my dad's example, I got to see firsthand what it looks like when you don't let the fear of what others think stand in the way. Even though friends and family members blasted him, even though they all told him he was foolish, he followed his heart anyway.

I'm not saying it was easy for him, or for me, to hear those harsh words. It is always more difficult when the critics of your dreams are those closest to you. We are all emotional people who want to be accepted by others—especially by those who seem to know us best. But sometimes even those who ought to stand by your side will end up being the first in line to shoot you down. That's when your resolve is truly tested.

I'm not suggesting that you ignore the advice of those who love you. In most cases, you will have their support when they see that you are committed to something. What I am saying is that you cannot make the approval of others—even those closest to you—a prerequisite for pursuing what you believe in. If something is deep in your heart and you know it's the right thing to do, you don't need a show of hands to get you moving. Just move yourself.

In the end, my dad held fast to his belief and pointed that borrowed car toward Atlanta despite knowing his friends and family thought he was crazy at best and terribly irresponsible at worst. And in the end, my dad's actions saved my mom's life.

It would be an interesting experiment if you could somehow jump ahead a few years and observe what your life would look like if you didn't fear what other people thought, and then also observe what it would look like if you did. Something like this actually happened to a man named Wes Moore. He wrote a book about the experience called *The Other Wes Moore*. The story goes like this.

In December 2000, the *Baltimore Sun* ran a short article about Moore who, at the time, was a local student who had just received a prestigious Rhodes Scholarship. Wes bought a copy of the paper to save as a keepsake.

After he read the article about himself, he skimmed over the rest of the paper and discovered an article about four young men who had killed a police officer in a failed armed robbery. What stuck out to him was that one of the young men was also named Wes Moore.

As the author says on his book website, he couldn't shake the coincidence that two young men with the same name were appearing in the same paper for completely opposite reasons—one to be celebrated for his success, the other to be condemned for his failure.

Moore followed the story of the other Wes Moore, who was eventually convicted of murder and sentenced to life in prison. He wrote a letter to the other young man who shared his name, asking him how it all happened. That letter initiated a relationship that lasted for several years and led to an eye-opening discovery. The two Wes Moores had almost parallel lives. They both had tough childhoods in similar neighborhoods. Both were father-less. Both hung out with the wrong crowd and had run-ins with the police when they were young. However, their lives had clearly diverged on one specific point—their re-actions to peer pressure. The celebrated Wes Moore had eventually chosen to ignore what the wrong crowd said he should do. He didn't fear what they thought of him. The convicted Wes Moore had chosen to listen to the wrong crowd and comply. He was more concerned with being accepted than doing what was best for his life. The results clearly spoke for themselves.[2]

•••

The fear of what people think holds many people back from pursuing their dreams. Don't feel like something is wrong with you if you've ever thought about the words of others. It's in our nature to care what other people think about us. But understand that there is a huge difference between caring about what other people think and fearing what they think. It is very possible to care what others think without letting their thoughts dictate your actions. It is nearly impossible to fear what other people think and keep that from hindering your progress. In fact, if you don't get the tendency in check, the fear will derail you altogether as it did the "other" Wes Moore.

Peer pressure, and the desire to be liked and accepted and to "fit in" are powerful forces. When you are young, they are typically the most powerful forces in your life. You have to know how to handle them if you are serious about reaching your dreams. That starts by understanding that no matter what you do and where you're trying to go, people will always have their opinions. And that's okay because that's all they are—opinions. Words floating in the air that have no power except the power you give them. Choose to only give power to your own words and the words of those whom you trust.

As for the rest of those words?

Let them drift to the ground where they can do you no harm.

[2] From www.theotherwesmoore.com and the book *The Other Wes Moore*, published in 2010 by Spiegel & Grau.

14

EXCUSES ARE A SIGN OF WEAKNESS

EXCUSES ARE A SIGN OF WEAKNESS

When I transferred to Detroit Catholic Central after my sophomore year in high school, I had no idea of the level of expectation that would be required of me from Coach Holowicki. For the majority of my childhood, I had seen my mom give in to the pressures of life and turn to alcohol and drugs for her escape. She seemed to always take the easy way out and find an excuse when things got tough. I didn't realize it, but some of the same traits that I watched in her as I was growing up had unknowingly taken root in me.

I'll never forget the time when the thought of taking the easy way out first surfaced in my life. It was the summer before my junior year. I was at a basketball camp that was held at our high school for elementary-aged kids in our area. The varsity team was required to do ball-handling demonstrations for the campers. As good of an athlete as I was, I had a glaring weakness when it came to my basketball game. I couldn't dribble very well with my left hand, and I had become very good at hiding it and just playing to my strengths.

The ball-handling drills started as usual on the right-hand side of the court, and I was putting on a show for the campers. Coach Holowicki barked out to everyone in the gym, "Whatever we do with our right hand, we have to be able to do it with our left hand too." Deep down, I knew I was in trouble. The drills began on the left side, and I dribbled off my foot and the ball rolled out of bounds. I picked it up and started again, only to lose control of the ball a second time. I was embarrassed, so I started limping and acting like I had pulled my hamstring and was injured. I walked off the court and headed to the training room.

I was so relieved to be off the court, but as soon as I reached the training room, I noticed Coach Holowicki and an assistant coach had followed me in. They asked the trainer to leave and quickly shut the door behind him. I'll never forget what happened next. Coach Holo-wicki got in my face and asserted, "I know you are new here at school, and you have a difficult time at home. But you need to get one thing straight. We don't make excuses here. You weren't injured. You were embarrassed because you can't dribble with your left hand. Because you're weak in that area, you made an excuse. Don't ever do that again. We don't find excuses. We find a way."

The greatest people in your life are those who expect you to do things you don't think you can do. When it came to dribbling with my left hand, Coach was relentless on me for the next two years of my high school career. By the time I graduated, my left hand was no longer a weakness.

•••

One of my biggest challenges growing up was learning to own the life I'd been given. That may sound like a no-brainer as you listen to my story. After all, I had no choice in all the experiences of those early years. But the truth is that everybody experiences things they didn't choose.

Many people spend the rest of their lives protesting and rebelling against the injustices of their past. They fill their minds with a long list of excuses for not chasing their dreams.

Others choose to own their lives and rise above their circumstances regardless of what happened.

One of the keys to bouncing back from adversity is accepting responsibility for your future, in thick and thin. That doesn't mean you remain where you are. And it doesn't mean you downplay negative circumstances or act like you enjoyed every moment you've been alive. What it does mean is that you reach a point where you admit, "Nobody but me can make something of my life." It's ultimately an admission that you have no excuses for not giving your all to be successful.

In the end, excuses are a sign of weakness. We all have reasons—some of them very legitimate reasons—to stop pursuing our dreams. I must have had a couple thousand before I reached middle school. So did Wendy and my mom and dad. You might too. But you can't let your reasons for quitting dictate what you do. Instead of spending time wallowing in your past, you have to spend time finding a way to a brighter future.

There is a critical difference between acknowledging your potential excuses and accepting them. To achieve your dreams, you have to understand this difference.

Accepting excuses is the same as accepting that you have no say in the outcome of your life. It is accepting that the negative forces in your life will always push you around and have the final say. It is accepting that your life will be defined by your circumstances and what others say about you. This is a tragic surrender because your excuses are the furthest thing from the truth about you or your potential.

There is a far better way to approach your potential excuses. Acknowledge them but refuse to accept them. It is healthy to acknowledge your potential excuses for not pursuing your dreams. Essentially, it is acknowledging that your dreams have enemies. More than that, it is calling out your dreams' enemies by name so they can be defeated specifically and purposefully.

Remember this: There is no such thing as a hero without a villain and a vast challenge to overcome. We idolize heroes because they are the kings and queens of the comeback. They illustrate that, no matter what you are up against, no matter how lopsided the odds, you can still come out on top.

Heroes don't become heroes because they don't

have excuses. Heroes become heroes because they don't accept the excuses they know they have. They merely acknowledge them and then find a way to rise above them. In doing so they remind us that it's never too late to be the hero of your own story.

A man named Walter Beran had every excuse in the world to not be successful. For starters, he was born three years before the Great Depression. And if he was superstitious, he had the additional misfortune of sharing his birthday, April 20, with one of the most evil men in history, Adolf Hitler. As if that wasn't a bad enough start, when Walter was eighteen months old, his dad went crazy and shot his mom and her brother-in-law, killing the brother-in-law and seriously injuring his mom. His dad was taken away and placed in a psychiatric hospital where he remained until the day he died. Walter never saw his father again. In fact, for most of his childhood he was raised by a woman he barely knew. Once his mom finally recovered from her injuries and returned home, she struggled with depression.

The house they lived in was a tiny shack with a large crack down the middle of the floor that reached from one corner of the room to the other. To make ends meet, Walter had to pick cotton for hours on end with his brothers, beginning when he was only five years old. Somehow he survived until he was old enough to enlist in the Army during World War II. He was promptly sent to England as an eighteen year old where he soon boarded a ship called the U.S.S. *Leopoldville* to cross the English Channel. The ship was torpedoed by a German submarine and sank. More than eight hundred soldiers were killed. Walter was found floating face up, nearly frozen in the forty-degree water. When he finally came to, he was in a French hospital screaming for help.

All this happened before Walter was nineteen years old. And none of this was Walter's fault. He was born into poverty at a time when the country was on the verge of the Great Depression. His father was a murderer who was gone before he could even say his name. His mother disappeared too, for more than a year to recover from injuries his father had inflicted on her. As a result, Walter was forced to live with people who weren't family and work long days in the cotton fields while he was just a kindergartener. Then, when he tried to do something good with his life, his ship was torpedoed. In an instant, he lost dozens of friends and nearly his own life.

I think few people would blame him if he just called it quits on life and became a bitter cynic or an alcoholic. However, that's not what he did.

Walter Beran became an incredibly grateful person who went on to be one of the top executives at one of the largest accounting firms in the world, a company called Ernst & Young. He was also the driving force behind rebuilding Los Angeles after the Watts Riots, and he became the point man responsible for helping Japanese businesses like Toyota, Mitsubishi and Nissan to flourish in America. He also advised three U.S. presidents on business matters in the United States, and he became close friends with Ronald and Nancy Reagan.

Walter had every excuse to strive for nothing but survival. He even had a compelling argument that life was out to get him. Yet, instead of finding excuses for not succeeding, he found a way around them and became a success in whatever he did.

In the end, excuses are the nails used to build a house of failure. It's okay to acknowledge they are there, but to be successful and achieve your dreams you have to learn to not pick them up.

People who succeed do what they say they are going to do. People who fail make excuses for falling short.

Excuses are a sign of weakness, and they pave the road to failure.

Excellence is a sign of strength, and it paves the road to success. Drop the excuses and embrace excellence at every turn.

15

MAKE YOUR WEAKNESSES YOUR STRENGTH

MAKE YOUR WEAKNESSES YOUR STRENGTH

My first speaking opportunity after walking away from professional basketball was not exactly a smashing success. Four people showed up. I went ahead with my speech anyway. I pursued similar opportunities in the weeks that followed, speaking to smaller crowds and sharing my heart, but the more I spoke the more I could sense I still had a lot to learn. While I was told I had a natural ability in front of a crowd, I didn't know what it took to truly connect to an audience. I knew my stories themselves were captivating, but I hadn't even considered learning more about the audience to whom I was speaking in order to tailor my words to their specific experiences and needs. I was just up there telling a story. I didn't yet know the impact I could have if I learned how to take the audience on a journey with me in order to help them learn the lessons I learned.

That's when I decided I should try to contact the best of the best at speaking to students in public schools throughout America. I found the number of a man named Dave Roever and sat down to call him.

Eight months into his duty in Vietnam, Dave was burned beyond recognition when a phosphorous grenade he was poised to throw exploded in his hand. Both his survival and his life since then are powerful and inspiring. Using his experiences of loneliness, peer pressure, disfigurement and pain as a backdrop for life lessons, Dave had shared his story with millions of students. I knew he could help me.

On our first phone call, Dave caught my vision. He must have heard my passion through the line. He invited me to spend a day with him and his wife, Brenda, at their ranch in Texas. To my surprise, during our time together Dave offered to let me travel with him for three months. It was the opportunity I needed.

On the road, he trained me in authority, leadership, humility and the importance of preparation. I was a sponge soaking up every bit of knowledge and insight he offered me. He also gave me more than advice. He actively demonstrated his belief in my newfound purpose by letting me have as much as thirty minutes of his hour-long assembly programs. I quickly learned to pour into students with all my heart and leave them with the life-changing lessons I had learned through my experiences.

Soon after the stint on the road with Dave, I was off and running on my own. But that progress never would have happened if I had not been willing to admit the areas where I was weak in communication and then sought to turn them into strengths.

Ray Kroc, the man who took McDonald's from a small operation to worldwide fame, once said that one of the keys to success was getting in the habit of finding another weakness to work on the moment after you succeeded at something. It's a great strategy for pursuing your dreams.

There is no doubt you'll have bumps in the road that arise from things you can't control. But the biggest bumps in the road are those inside you. You are your biggest hurdle to overcome. If you aren't willing to uncover and acknowledge the areas in which you are weak, and then work on improving them, you will place a ceiling on your potential. You'll be saying, "I'm only going to get as far as my current strengths will take me." That's like a musician saying she'll only play songs with the notes she knows—but not all the others. Or it's like a basketball player saying he's content just being a great free-throw shooter—never mind jump shots, dribbling, passing and defense. Or it's like a homebuilder confessing he's content to build houses with only a hammer and nails—never mind the other tools.

The truth is that the moment you stop trying to find ways to improve is the moment you've stepped off the road to success and onto the road to failure.

If you put in the hard work, you will eventually excel at something that comes naturally, whether it's a particular subject in school, a particular sport or a specific instrument. Maybe you've already discovered that thing at which you excel.

When you reach that point, you're faced with a

choice: You can celebrate the accomplishment and stay right there, or you can seek a new skill that complements the skill you currently possess. Do you remember the line I shared earlier in the book? If you keep doing what you've always done, you'll keep getting what you've always gotten. That's as true for success as it is for failure.

If you're happy with your current level of success, or you feel that whatever strengths you currently have can carry you to your biggest dreams, then by all means, stop growing. But if you want more for your life, then you need to learn to get more from yourself. That takes a commitment to constant improvement, a commitment to working on not only improving your current strengths but also making your current weaknesses new strengths.

There's been a lot of talk in recent years about the importance of discovering your strengths and focusing solely on using them to be successful. Discovering your strengths is critical to success, but hinging your continued success on a finite skill set is shortsighted and, frankly, very dangerous.

If I had subscribed to the notion that the pursuit of my dreams was all about finding and then focusing on my strengths, I'd still be trying to play basketball. Not only would that be sad at my current age; that would likely mean I'd be out of a career by now. Even if I wanted to stay in the sport of basketball, as a broadcaster or coach for instance, I couldn't do that without learning new skills. Dribbling, shooting, dunking, passing—these skills are not going to make me a great broadcaster. And while they will help me understand what a team needs to do to be successful, those skills don't have anything to do with being a great motivator and teacher like a good coach must be.

At some point along the path to your dreams, you're going to need more than you currently possess—especially if you plan on expanding your dreams throughout your life.

Consider Janet Robinson, who was a public school teacher for a decade before taking a sales management job with *The New York Times* Company. Today, she is the company's CEO. Do you think her strengths in teaching were the same strengths that allowed her to excel in sales management and eventually the leadership of a multi-billion dollar enterprise? No, she had to add new strengths at every new opportunity.

Or what about Martha Stewart? She wasn't always blessed with the knack for good food and great home décor. Before she became the household name she is today, she was a stockbroker, and then a caterer. Eventually her catering business opened her eyes to the bigger opportunity that is now her current empire, which includes a television show, a magazine, dozens of books and a home and garden product line sold through K-Mart.

There is simply no truth to the notion that you can keep reaching higher and higher in life with the same strengths you've always had. While it's important to continue applying your strengths at every opportunity, the only way you will be able to seize new and bigger opportunities is to identify your weaknesses and then commit to making them your strengths. It takes persistence. Once your weakness becomes your strength, find another weakness. This cycle never stops for the highest achievers.

16

WHO YOU SURROUND YOURSELF WITH IS WHO YOU EVENTUALLY BECOME

WHO YOU EVENTUALLY BECOME
WHO YOU SURROUND YOURSELF WITH IS

If there's one thing my tumultuous upbringing taught me, it was that going with the flow gets you nowhere. It is a false foundation, like quicksand or a partially frozen lake. Growing up, I learned to quickly evaluate my surroundings and find the highest ground. Life was rarely safe, so I had to find stability wherever and with whomever I could. One place I never found it was in chasing after cool.

Trying to please the crowd forces you to follow the crowd and even encourages you to remain average just like the crowd. Sometimes the biggest enemy of your dreams is not difficult circumstances or difficult people who clearly stand against you. Sometimes the biggest enemy of your dreams is the strong pull to be accepted by your peers, especially the people you call your friends.

In the end, you have to make your own rules about what is acceptable in order for you to achieve your dreams. One of my rules was that I wasn't going to get caught up with alcohol, smoking or drugs—no matter what. We all make mistakes and I was no exception. But the difference for me was that I knew the real dangers of partying and what it eventually could lead to. It helped me quickly bounce back up from my mistakes and make up my mind to not let it happen again. Even though some of my friends and teammates thought partying made them cool, I knew that opening the door to the party life was to invite disaster.

That decision made me stick out like a sore thumb on many occasions, especially when it was a good time to celebrate, and especially when it meant saying no to a guy named David. He was the most popular guy in my high school. He was good looking and loved by all the girls. He threw epic parties, and he had all the hookups for alcohol and drugs.

He pressured everybody. One day he approached me and asked if I was coming to his party. I told him no, and I explained that I'd seen alcohol and drugs destroy my family, that I had made the mistake before and I couldn't invite more of that into my life. As soon as I said those things, I prepared myself for the backlash. I figured he'd laugh at me or call over some other friends and give me a hard time. But that's not what happened at all.

Just when I thought David was going to make fun of me, I saw that my words made him gain a greater respect for me. It is still a vivid memory because I know that one particular decision could have derailed me. If I'd chosen to be David's friend and go along with what he was doing, it might have made me more popular but it would have probably destroyed my chance at the dreams that were in my heart.

Growing up around my mom helped me learn at a very young age that a person's friends play a big role in his or her future. Her so-called friends were the most consistent reason she struggled with her addictions. They were also the primary source of instability, fear and danger in our house. My mom's friends were druggies, alcoholics and abusers. In other words, she chose to surround herself with losers that did nothing but drag her down. This choice was the main reason she remained a loser herself and could not rise above her circumstances for so long.

•••

The one area that can always keep you from reaching your potential is the company you keep. The people you hang around either lift you up or drag you down. My mom's company was relentlessly dragging her down. And when I was with her—when I was in *her* company—I was also dragged down.

Over time I began to see more clearly the two roads before me: One that was leading to the death of my dreams, and one that was leading to the fulfillment of my dreams. As much as it hurt my heart, I already knew as a high school student that if my mom didn't change the company she kept, I would have to break free from her as soon as I was able.

Most of us have been taught from a young age

through various character development programs that we should always be unselfish. I agree with this as it pertains to most aspects of life. However, there is one area in which I am convinced everyone should be self-ish. If you are ever going to reach your dreams, you have to be selfish about who you allow into your life. Show me your friends, goes the saying, and I'll show you your future.

The friendships you allow into your life play a huge role in the path your life takes. They will either make you or break you. If you are serious about becoming successful and reaching your dreams, you have to make a choice on who comes with you. You don't need people in your life that make you feel good because they tell you what you want to hear. What you need are people in your life who believe in who you can become—people who will challenge you to be the best you can possibly be.

You've no doubt heard the phrase "guilty by asso-ciation." It's a phrase based on the notion that just be-cause one person is hanging out with another person who is doing something illegal, that first person must be doing something illegal too. Ironically, from a legal standpoint a person cannot be convicted in a court be-cause they were simply in the wrong place at the wrong time. But that's just the legal point of view. When it comes to the social point of view, the phrase "guilty by association" is often foolproof, especially when talking about people who have been friends for more than a couple of weeks.

If your friends are doing things that would land

them in deep water with your parents or school or local authorities, and you continue hanging out with them, it will be next to impossible for you to not eventually do what they do. Or, in the least, it will be very difficult for you to prove to others that you are different and hold yourself to a higher standard.

Consider the case of a sixteen-year-old Texas boy named Tony Sparks who allowed himself to be involved with some older friends who were in a gang. On June 20, 1999, two of these friends invited him to meet with them and plan what they considered was a small-scale robbery. Their plan was to ask someone in a parking lot for a ride and then get in that person's car and pull out a gun. From there they would steal the person's money and personal belongings, obtain their ATM pin, and then lock him or her in the trunk and abandon the car.

The next day, Sparks hopped in the car with his friends, and they picked up two more gang members to help with their plan. The group of five got their hands on two pistols and set out in search of a victim.

Sometime during the afternoon of June 21, the five pulled into the parking lot of a local convenience store in Killeen, Texas, where they found a man named Todd using a pay phone.

The man and his wife, Stacie, were in town visiting old friends whom they had gotten to know when Todd was stationed at nearby Fort Hood. They had just finished lunch with friends and had stopped briefly to make a call. While Todd used the pay phone, Stacie waited in the car. That's when Tony Sparks and one of the other four boys approached Todd and asked him for a ride to their uncle's house. Todd agreed and the two boys, along with a third who was standing nearby, slid into the backseat of the couple's car.

One of the boys gave the man directions, and then he immediately pulled out a .40 caliber handgun, pointed it at Todd's head and proclaimed, "The plans have changed."

He then ordered Todd to stop the car, at which point the three boys stole his wallet, his wife's purse and jewelry, and then forced the couple into the trunk of their car. While they drove to an ATM to withdraw money from their account, the boys' plan started unraveling.

Sparks and another boy were sitting in the back seat where they could hear the couple speaking to them from the trunk. The couple asked them to consider what they were doing and pleaded for their lives to be spared. By the time the three met back up with their other two friends, Sparks had had a change of heart. He didn't want to be part of the plan anymore.

The older boy driving the car ridiculed Sparks, but eventually dropped him off at his house. Then the older boy and the other remaining boy drove the couple's car to a remote area where they shot Todd and Stacie in the trunk and set their car on fire. The other two friends had provided the gasoline for the fire and were supposed to be the getaway car. But as they drove away, their car slid off the road and into a muddy ditch. Local police officers, who had been informed of a fire, arrived at the scene while the four boys were trying to push the getaway car out of the ditch. When firemen discovered the bodies in the trunk of the burning car, the four were immediately arrested.

In the months that followed, all four boys were tried and found guilty of a list of serious crimes ranging from robbery to kidnapping to murder. The two older boys—eighteen and nineteen years old at the time—were given death sentences.

As for the fifth friend, Tony Sparks, when the evidence came out that he had been with the other four boys up until the actual murder took place, he too had to stand trial. Today he is serving a life sentence without the chance for parole. Even though Tony Sparks came to his senses and walked away before things got really bad, the friendships he had already formed sealed his fate. He entered a Texas prison at sixteen and will likely never live outside those walls again.

His story serves as a harsh but very real reminder of what can happen when you choose the wrong friends. While a little misbehaving here and there may seem harmless now—if you continue to hang out with friends who are going in the opposite direction of your dreams, your life will eventually follow the same path no matter how much you want to succeed.

The best way to describe the impact of friendships is this: Who you surround yourself with is who you eventually become. One wrong friendship can completely alter the direction of your life. One right friendship can lift you higher than you can go alone.

Choose your friends wisely. To paraphrase an ancient Jewish proverb: If you walk with the wise you will grow wise, but if you're the friend of fools you will suffer harm.

17

BE TEACHABLE

BE TEACHABLE

Legend has it that after World War I, a London newspaper sent out a request to several prominent people of that time asking them to submit an essay answering the question: "What is wrong with the world?" A British writer named G. K. Chesterton was one of the people who received the request. He was known to be one of the greatest thinkers of the time and there's no doubt the newspaper's editor expected a long and thoughtful response. Instead Chesterton wrote back the following:

Dear Sirs,

In response to your question, "What is wrong with the world?"

I am.

Sincerely,

G. K. Chesterton

G. K. Chesterton was a highly accomplished man.

The most successful people of the time called him a genius. His novels inspired the minds and hearts of fellow writers like H. G. Wells who wrote *The War of the Worlds* and C. S. Lewis who penned the Narnia series. His regular column in another London newspaper was said to have had a major impact on Mahatma Gandhi, the leader who fought for and won freedom for the people of India.

If anyone was equipped to provide a long and eloquent answer to the question, "What is wrong with the world?" it was G. K. Chesterton. There's no question he already had the knowledge. Instead, he provided a two-word answer that revealed the secret to all his accomplishments. By admitting he was the problem with the world, he was acknowledging that he had not learned it all. In short, he was admitting he was still teachable.

• • •

Throughout my teens I was often reminded that I would never reach my dreams unless I continued improving in every aspect of my being. There was no room to regress into know-it-all mode or into some sort of arrogance that I already had everything it took to succeed. The truth was that as a teenager I wasn't even close—even though I was tall and could jump high. I still had a lot to learn before I could become the professional basketball player I wanted to be. And I definitely had a lot to learn to become the husband and father I wanted to be. Even today, after eighteen years of marriage and with two teenage kids of my own, I am still learning how to be a better husband and dad. And that's the key.

Remaining teachable means that you never really "arrive" in any important aspect of your life. While you can certainly reach a point where you are highly skilled and highly confident in your ability to produce great results, the moment you think you have everything you need is the moment you begin to falter.

Life is so unpredictable because we can never control every force around us. Our environment is constantly changing. Just when you think you have a grip on your future, something shifts. Maybe a parent gets sick, or maybe you sustain a severe injury and can no longer play your sport. Or maybe you didn't receive the scholarship for which you worked so hard, and you're going to have to find a job to pay for college.

Or like a businessman named Erik Wahl, maybe a recession forces you to rethink your dream in another career.[3] Erik co-owned a successful business for nearly ten years, only to have it crumble after the 2000 recession. With a wife and three kids under the age of four, and very little money in the bank, he didn't have the luxury of spending six months relaxing on the beach and hoping the next step came to him.

On a whim he went to an art supply store and picked up some paints, a few brushes and a couple of canvases. At the very least, he thought that painting would give him an outlet that would help reduce his stress. He'd always had an interest in art but he had no training whatsoever. In fact, the last time he had tried to paint something, his elementary teacher insisted that art was not his thing. But something inside him was still fascinated with painting.

Over the next few days, Erik's little stress-reducer started to become something much bigger. He found himself spending more and more time painting and studying new techniques and the history of the medium. He was soon hooked on art, and he poured all his energies into becoming a great artist.

Do you know what he's doing today, ten years later? He's not running a business. He's a highly sought-after graffiti artist who can paint a perfect likeness of a well-known face in about three minutes, upside down, before a live audience.

Do you know who his audiences are? Businesses, like the one he used to own, that are looking for ways to become more creative. If you were to ask Erik today if he wishes he had his old career back, he'd laugh. He knows that the unexpected path he followed ultimately led him to his dream job. But he would have never discovered it had he not remained teachable and continued to learn.

Britain's great Prime Minister Winston Churchill explained it best when he said, "To improve is to change; to be perfect is to change often." If you want to reach your dreams and sustain them for the rest of your life, the only thing you should know for sure is that you will never know everything you need to know. There will always be more opportunity for growth, sometimes where you least expect it, sometimes where you've been looking all along.

Be teachable. And stay that way.

[3] Erik Wahl, *Unthink*. Crown Business, 2013.

18

PASSION IS YOUR GREATEST ASSET

PASSION IS YOUR GREATEST ASSET

After I walked away from the only career I had known, I faced the reality that Kristie and I owned nothing—no car, no home—only the clothes on our backs and the hope and faith in our hearts. And I had no money coming in. Soon, the rent was due on our furnished apartment, and I had to figure out how I was going to make this bigger dream happen sooner than later.

I'd just made the craziest decision of my life. I'd chosen to leave a solid career at which I'd worked for nearly my entire life, and in its place I was going to try to establish myself in an industry where I had zero experience. The only crowd I had ever spoken to was a locker room of my own teammates. Besides that, I didn't have any promotional materials to send out, and I didn't even know whom to call.

Chad, listen, a voice in my head said, *you need to go back. You need to play. You know, play at least one more year and save up some money and then maybe this will make more sense. Otherwise, how are you gonna make it? Huh? You're supposed to be the man of the house, the provider. Now you don't even know how you're going to pay the rent. Call your agent back and tell him you just lost your head for a moment.*

Chasing my new dream wasn't easy. I knew it wouldn't be. But until I was standing there with my basketball career behind me and no safety net beneath me, I didn't realize how far from easy the path would truly be. I was unknown. I had no speaking contacts or booking agents. Whenever I called looking for opportunities, the receptionist wanted to know my qualifications. I had none. I only had a story—and a passion to help students get through their own challenges.

That passion—that core belief that I could truly help kids like me—drove me to keep calling despite the initial rejections and embarrassment. By then I knew what it took to bounce back from failure, and I kept bouncing until I finally learned what to say that would pique people's interest. "Just a few days ago," I began, "I gave up a lucrative career in professional basketball because I have a passion to help hurting kids like I once was. Some incredible things have happened in my life. Can you give me just ten minutes to share a little of it with you?"

With that brief but passionate introduction, people began to open their doors and listen to me pour out my heart. Soon I was scheduling speaking opportunities. I didn't ask if the crowds were big or small. It didn't matter to me. I just had to relay my story and the lessons I'd learned—to anyone, anywhere I could. And so I did.

Without any promotional material or experience, I booked three months' of speaking opportunities in just three days. Then, as I explained earlier, I met Dave Roever not long after I finished my first week of speaking. His investment into my life, combined with my heartfelt passion to share my story as often as possible, illuminated the path toward realizing my new dream.

In the end, the fuel that keeps you fired up about chasing your dreams is passion. While all these other lessons I've shared with you are critical to learn, the fact is that if you aren't passionate about your dreams, you'll eventually run out of steam.

There's a telltale sign that helps you determine whether your dream is something you're truly passionate about—I call it the litmus test of true dreams. Bring your dream to mind right now. Then ask yourself this question: *Do I think about this dream when I wake up each morning? Is it something I think about all the time?*

It might sound like an overly simple test, but the truth is that you can't fake passion. And if your dream is not truly your passion, you won't think about it when you wake up. You won't be excited about it all the time.

Let me pause here and say that it is good and perfectly normal to have hobbies that interest you and subjects that you enjoy from time to time. I have a handful of activities and topics that I'm interested in. But the difference between those things and my dream is simply mind space. I don't think about those other things even one-tenth as much as I think about sharing my story and communicating the lessons I've learned in my life with people like you.

Today I still enjoy basketball—it was obviously a major part of my life for a very long time. As a result, I'll catch a game on TV or attend one live when I can. But I care far less about watching that kind of game than watching my son, Cameron, throw a baseball or my daughter, Kiersten, spike a volleyball. My family is the greatest passion in my life. If I'm not thinking about offering my love, support and leadership to my wife and kids, then I'm thinking about ways that I can impact as many people as possible through speaking. Outside of those two activities—loving my family and reaching people through my story—there is nothing else that I'd call my passion. I've learned that the only way my life truly matters is if I can somehow take the pain of my past and use it to help others overcome the obstacles in their way.

Now the question comes back to you.

Do you wake up thinking about your dreams? If you don't, you need to dig deeper. And don't listen to the cynics. The only limit to your dreams is your own imagination. What are you truly passionate about? When you find your dream, the one that wakes you up in the morning excited, that's when you know you'll have the passion to see it through—and then continue to greater heights.

Passion will compel you to overcome adversity on the inside and outside. It will ensure that you see the world as a place of infinite potential and ripe with opportunity at every turn. It will protect you from the doubters and strengthen you against your own doubts. It will strip away the phony layers around you and bring out your best and brightest self. Ultimately, passion will make you a person who is always grateful for what you have been given. And grateful people are giving people.

In the end you will discover, as I did, that your biggest dreams always involve other people.

•••

Years into my new career, I was driving home from a speaking engagement with both kids, now no longer toddlers, in the back seat. I glanced in the rearview mirror. I caught an expression on Kiersten's face that made me think of Wendy. I am forever grateful Wendy remained by my side all through the years—especially when she was my only protector. She's happily married now and the mother of three precious girls of her own. As I'm sure you can imagine, she is an incredible wife and mom.

I looked at Cameron, and he asked me how long until we'd be home. I thought of my dad who had fielded that same question from me more times than could be counted. I felt a great sense of gratitude for a father who showed me what it means to serve others unconditionally. He remains an example today, not just for me but also for his grandkids.

Tears clouded my sight as I saw the innocence in the eyes of my kids who would never have to suffer through the unnecessary trauma of my childhood. I reflected on the ups and downs in my mom's life. Seeing her die and then come back to life. Witnessing her curled into a corner and convulsing from withdrawals. I marveled again at how we found her in Atlanta. I thought of how I had to release myself from feeling responsible for her. I prayed for her right then, as I had so many times. I was grateful I now had reason to celebrate her life.

• • •

A few years after my mom overdosed, I learned that while she was flat-lined she had a dream...

She was standing at the bottom of a slick, grassy hill when she noticed a bright light at the top. She began crawling toward the light. She clawed her way up and up and up until she couldn't climb any further. At the top of the hill, she came to a tall, wrought- iron fence that blocked her from the light just on the other side.

She went to talk but couldn't. Her lips were para-lyzed.

In her mind she cried out, "Please send me back! Please send me back!"

There was no response. Only silence.

She dropped her head into her hands and began to sob.

Then she was snapped back to life.

• • •

It would take a great fight from my mom to make something of that second chance. For a long time it seemed she was wasting the opportunity, like she'd wasted all the others before.

But somehow she kept fighting. Every time she got knocked down, she got back up. Eventually, she started to find her own inner strength. She began to taste success.

Gradually, my mom rose higher and higher above her mistakes and circumstances. She had her struggles along the way, but she kept bouncing back, and bouncing higher.

Eventually, she beat down her demons for good.

Today she enjoys her five grandchildren—my two and Wendy's three—without the guilt or fear of leaving them scarred. And she can pass along to them those captivating qualities that my dad saw in her at the very beginning—when she was still a teenager.

Best of all, our relationship has been restored. My mom travels with me to speaking events as often as she can. It is the most unlikely of bonds, but it was made possible because we both refused to give up. We refused to give up on ourselves. And we refused to give up hope that life could be better than the one we'd been born into.

Ultimately, we refused to stop chasing our dreams.

FINAL THOUGHTS

FINAL THOUGHTS

I've now spoken thousands of times to millions of students and adults alike. The more I speak, the more I realize that my story isn't as rare as I once thought. I am approached on a regular basis with stories so horrific I sometimes wonder how that person is still standing before me.

Maybe you've been reading this book and you're just like one of those people, hurting from a life of constant fear, abandonment and pain. Or maybe you know somebody like that. The urgency of helping hurting people burns within me, and I want you to know, more than anything else you've heard, that if I made it, you can too. I also want you to know that you can still achieve great things. Your past is no predictor of your future when passion lights your way. Reignite your dreams and bounce after them.

My heart also goes out to anyone who has given into

the lie that alcohol, drugs or abuse are the way to escape life's pain. If that's you, I want you to receive this message of encouragement that it doesn't have to be that way. There is a greater purpose for your life.

It may not seem that way now, but I can promise you that one day you'll look back on your life and realize that there is something significant about it all—something bigger and greater than you realized back then. You can either choose to seek it now and then chase after it. Or you can choose to sit back and let life happen to you. Either way, you are making a choice. I hope you will choose to pursue the life you were meant to live. It's always there for you to discover. The path to purpose won't always be easy, but it will always be rewarding. No step you take in the direction of your dreams will bring you regret.

At some point, you've probably heard somebody say, "What goes up must come down." Unfortunately, the opposite is not also true.

What goes down does not always come back up.

Life can be hard, like the polished wood of a basketball court. Your mistakes and circumstances can throw you down, sometimes far too many times. When that happens, you can begin to feel deflated, defeated and useless. These same emotions keep a lot of people down. Many never get back up. But that won't be you—because now you know how to bounce.

Your passionate dreams are the air to your existence. They are why you are here. Listen to them and let them fill your circumstances with hope, determination and faith so that whenever life throws you down, you have the strength and enthusiasm to rise. Then follow their lead as they inspire you to soar higher and higher than you ever imagined. This ride is why you are alive.

It is never, ever too early or too late to chase your dreams. They are real and they matter. They are the truest things in your life and mine. We are all made to accomplish something great—your dreams form your unique compass for doing just that. Choose to follow them no matter the cost. And remember this when things don't go your way:

Down is inevitable.

Up is a choice.

A NOTE FROM MY MOM

A NOTE FROM MY MOM

'll leave you with the words my mom wrote to me after reading the story you just read for the first time. They will remind you that no matter how difficult life gets, as long as you have breath there is still hope.

Dear Chad,

I stared at the package on my kitchen table for days. I finally opened it with more fear and anxiety than anyone could possibly imagine. The idea of my dreadful life of selfishness and child abuse in full print for the whole world to read seemed more than I could bear. And then I found your note:

"Dear Mom, I know this is going to be difficult for you to read but I want you to remember that I love you with all of my heart. Our story should have ended in tragedy but, instead, it has become a source of hope and inspiration to millions of people. I am proud of you mom and I am proud to be your son. I love you, Chad."

As I opened the book and began to read, tears immediately filled my eyes. Many of the stories were like a dream. I was strung out on drugs and alcohol, or in a blackout state so much of the time. But the more I read the more I began to remember and relive those horrifying events. The things I put my children through. The terrible, selfish life I led. And yet here was my son saying, "Mom, It's okay, I love you." What a precious son. I wept bitterly. It's hard to believe that a child could forgive a mother as heartless as me. You see, no one realizes more than me that I do not deserve your forgiveness or love. To this day it is hard for me to understand and I do not take it for granted for a single moment.

Everyday, when I see little children, especially my grandchildren, with parents that watch their every move, never leaving their side, laughing at every funny little thing they do, staying up with them all night when they are sick, making a big deal of the first picture they drew and taking pictures of the silliest events in their lives...I am reminded of you and Wendy. And I can't help but think, "Everything I could have been and all that my children should have had was stolen from them." But those demons I battled nearly everyday of my life did not win in the end.

I will forever be thankful that you, your sister and father never ever gave up on me through my endless years of struggles and failures. You believed in me when I had no faith in myself, you forgave me when I could not forgive myself, you encouraged me when I had no hope and you loved me until I was able to love myself.

No son, this book is not difficult for me to read. It is the greatest achievement of my life. And I hope that somehow, in some miraculous way, our story will remind others that they too can find the strength, no matter what they face, to never ever give up.

I love you my son,

Mom

For more information on The Chad Varga Company
or booking the author to speak, please email to:
booking@chadvarga.com.

ABOUT THE AUTHOR

ABOUT THE AUTHOR

Chad is the founder and president of The Chad Varga Company, and has established a national reputation for his authentic and undeniable ability to relate to teenagers and inspire them to pursue their dreams regardless of their circumstances. He has spoken to more than three million students throughout America and has been a featured guest on many of America's major television and radio networks. Chad was named one of six up-and-coming leaders in America by *New York Times* Bestselling Author, Dr. John Maxwell and was nominated as one of the REAL Richest People In America for his work with Students.

Chad and his wife Kristie are the proud parents of two children, their son Cameron and daughter Kiersten.

Like: facebook.com/chadvarga

Follow: @chadvarga